Dirty, Dave's 101
X-RATED
JOKES

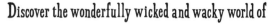

Discover the wonderfully wicked and wacky world of

Dirty, Dave's 101
X-RATED
JOKES

Illustrated by Peter Bramley

BELL PUBLISHING COMPANY
NEW YORK

This 1983 edition is published by Bell Publishing Company,
One Park Avenue, New York, New York 10016

Manufactured in the United States of America

Library of Congress Cataloging in Publication Data

Shumaker, David.
  Dirty Dave's 101 x-rated jokes.
    1. Sex—Anecdotes, facetiae, satire, etc. I. Title.
II. Title: Dirty Dave's 101 x-rated jokes.
PN6231.S54S48   1983   818'.5402   82-20643
ISBN: 0-517-403005
h g f e d c b

CONTENTS

PREFACE

Is nothing sacred? Not to the lover of the dirty joke. And the joke's on you. And you are the priest, the virgin, the newlywed, the cuckold, the homosexual, the necrophile, the coward, the cripple, the innocent, the guilty, and the insufferable snob. No institution is invulnerable to the dissecting scalpel of the dirty joke. Shock, surprise, double entendre, innuendo (Italian for Preparation H™), and undisguised obscenity are all elements of the dirty joke. All elements with which man tries to reduce to a manageable size his highly complex, confusing, frustrating, satisfying, and silly sexuality.

"Smut," said Freud, "unfailingly produces a cheerful mood among the common people." Laugh, clown, laugh, but the joke's always at someone's expense and hopefully at someone else's. The dirty joke as counterculture has flourished and continues to flourish even in today's permissive society because of man's unique ability and need to laugh at himself. The dirty joke as a creative form passes quickly into the public domain as none can claim absolute paternity. And in the public domain dirty jokes are told, retold, and kept alive by that "cheerful mood among the common people."

Dirty Dave's 101 X-Rated Jokes contains old jokes (where did they come from?) and new jokes (where do they come from?). Undoubtedly some have appeared in print in different versions at some point in time. But I cheerfully submit my distinctive renderings for your prurient perusal and heartily applaud past, present, and future anthologies that have helped and will help stabilize, but not sanitize, the dirty joke as art form.

Dirty Dave

New York City
1983

Dirty, Dave's 101 X-RATED JOKES

Chief Crazy Chicken

Chief Crazy Chicken was tired of the local stuff at the reservation and decided to go into the white man's town and get himself a white man's woman. He didn't have much difficulty finding the house on the wrong side of the tracks with the red light in the window. The madam received him and said, "Well, hello, Chief, what can I do for you?"

"Hmmm, me heap big Indian chief. Me want to fuckum white woman."

"I can understand that, Chief, but do you have any wampum?"

"Hmmm, me got plenty wampum."

"Sorry, Chief, you have to have a lot more wampum than that to touch one of my girls. Now let me tell you what you do. Go back to the reservation, stick your dick in a tree for a year, save your money, and then come back to see me."

A year later Chief Crazy Chicken again mounted his pony and rode into the white man's town. "Well, hello, Chief," greeted the madam, "I remember you. Did you do like I told you and save up your wampum?"

"Hmmm, me plenty big Indian chief, got plenty big wampum. Me want to fuckum white woman."

"Yes, well, I can see that you do. Hey, Stella, take the chief here up to Room Four. Listen, Chief, Rosie's up there. Just tell her what you want and it's yours."

Chief Crazy Chicken liked Rosie a lot and told her to strip naked and get on the bed on her hands and knees facing away from him. Then he took off his belt, looped one end around his hand, and popped her a smart one across the ass. "Jesus Christ!" yelled Rosie. "What'd you do that for?"

"Hmmm, me checkum knothole for bees first!"

Game Time

His wife accompanied him on the business trip against his wishes, but after dinner in a fine restaurant and a pleasant evening at the theater, his mood had mellowed, and he almost felt amiable when they arrived back at their hotel room. He glanced out the window and happened to see a couple across the air shaft. His attention became riveted.

"George, what are you doing, George?" whined his wife, a perennial whiner.

"I'm looking at the couple across the air shaft."

"George, what are they doing, George?"

"As best I can tell, he's trying to pitch grapes into her snatch, and she's trying ring-a-rosy-oh with doughnuts on his dick. Want to give it a try?"

"Sure, George, sure. Pass me the lifesavers."

At Harvard

Bubba was bopping across the greensward at Harvard when he encountered a buttoned-down senior classman.

"Hey, there, honky bro', where the library be at?"

Shriveling with disdain, the senior classman replied, "Are you addressing me?" And he continued on his way.

"Hey, wait a minute, little white buddy," said Bubba as he fell in step alongside the Harvard man. "All I want to know is where the library be at."

"Firstly," sneered the senior classman, "I am not your honky bro'. Secondly, I am not your little white buddy. And thirdly, we at Harvard do not end our sentences with prepositions."

"Sho' nuff?" said Bubba. "Well, excuse me all to hell. Where the library be at, asshole!"

Justice!

"I demand to see the senator!"

"Who shall I say is calling, sir?"

"The grim reaper, the hand of God, Justice!"

"Excuse me, Senator, there's a gentleman here to see you. Well, he says he's the grim reaper, the hand of God, and Justice! Yes, Senator. Sir, the senator wants to know if you represent a rock group."

"Tell the senator I represent virginity!"

At that moment the senator cautiously peeked from his office, then broke into a broad smile.

"Ah, Mr. Ferndicker, why didn't you say it was you? Please, come right in."

When they were behind the closed door, Mr. Ferndicker launched into a tirade.

"How dare you sit there, you complacent, smug fat-cat! My daughter's pregnant! And don't try to deny you did it, you cradle robber, you despoiler of youth. You millionaire politicians are all alike. Nothing but teeth and dick! Smile for the cameras and slam the pork into every young innocent with stars in her eyes! I want justice! What're you going to do about it?!"

"Please, sit, calm down, Mr. Ferndicker. I'm perfectly willing to accept my responsibility. That was my campaign slogan, you know, 'Call Me Responsible!' If your daughter has a boy, I will give her one hundred thousand dollars. If it's a girl, a hundred and fifty thousand. I'm partial to girls, you know."

The anger melted from Mr. Ferndicker's face and was replaced by doubt.

"And if she has a miscarriage," he said, "would you give her a second chance?"

Mommy's Black Sponge

Little Tommy burst through the bathroom door without knocking and surprised his mother standing naked in the tub toweling herself dry. His eyes immediately riveted on the thick bush of dark hair between her legs. "What's that?" Tommy cried with the enthusiasm of discovery.

"Oh, ah, I, ah, oh, that's my black sponge," recovered Tommy's mother.

Apparently satisfied with that explanation, he went about his business until a few days later when he rushed into the kitchen with his little playmate Joey. "Mommy, Mommy, Joey wants to see your black sponge."

"Oh, I, ah, oh, I lost it," Tommy's quick-thinking mother offered.

Tommy was disappointed, but disappointment is easily forgotten by little boys. And so apparently was the black sponge until some time later when Tommy, flushed with delight, again rushed in to his mother, "Mommy, Mommy, I found your black sponge. The maid's cleaning Daddy's face with it!"

Luck of the Irish

The leprechaun appeared in front of him on the third green and said, "Ah, what is it you might be wishin' for? A wee crock of gold?"

The astonished golfer answered, "You're . . ."

"My what?" snapped the leprechaun. "You can't be taking anything that's mine, don't you know. One wish I can grant you, but you'll have nary a thing that's me own."

"I . . . I . . . I'd like a better golf game," stammered

the golfer. "Better than that, I'd like a superb golf game."

"Ah, so a superb golf game is what you'd be askin' for. Sure I am that I can grant you that, but you must realize to get a superb golf game, you'll be havin' to give something up."

"What?"

"Well, a little thing, really, just a little bit of your sex life 'tis all."

"It's a deal," replied the golfer.

A year later the same leprechaun appeared on the third green before the same golfer and said, "Ah, now is it a superb golf game you've been havin' this year past?"

"More than superb," said the grateful golfer. "I don't seem to be able to do anything wrong with a golf club."

"And your sex life? Did you mind losing that little bit I told you about?" asked the leprechaun.

"Not in the least."

"And how many times did you make love this year past, if I might ask."

"Three times."

"Only three times? Why that's a dreadful score!"

"Oh, I don't know," replied the golfer. "It's not so bad for a priest stuck in a small parish!"

Not for the Abbey

"Now," said the abbot, glowering over the twenty feet of cold stone floor at the eight young men lined up against the wall in front of him, "you think you want to leave the realm of worldly pleasures and join our monastery. A lusty-looking bunch of young scoundrels, if you ask me—not a pious eye to be had among the lot of you. Strip naked and pile your clothes neatly on the floor in front of me."

The hapless young men quickly did as they were told and scampered back across the stone floor to their position against the wall.

"Brother Michael," ordered the abbot, "position the bells." Brother Michael carefully tied a small silver bell with a piece of silk cord around the penis of each young man.

"Now," said the abbot with a throaty, malicious laugh, "we'll see just how pious your eyes are. Any man of you who rings his bell will leave immediately, never to return. Brother Michael, fetch the wretched slattern in."

A lovely girl with sunset-flame hair, wide-set green eyes, a pert upturned nose, and a body that paled the great Aphrodite's form entered. She approached the eight young men, eyeing them suggestively, and began to taunt their young manhood with her body, which she also began to uncover for them. She cupped her naked breasts, stroked her creamy, taut thighs, and undulated before them, until finally one tiny silver bell tinkled slowly at first, then faster and faster until it sprang up and quivered, tinkling in the air.

"Silly Peter," said the abbot disgustedly, "you are not for our world. Get your clothes and leave this place."

The abbot began to praise the remaining seven young men for their purity and chaste hearts, but as the abject and embarrassed young Peter bent over to gather his clothes, the abbot was drowned out by the furious tinkling of seven tiny silver bells!

The Foreign Legion

Three lusty Foreign Legionnaires were captured by a powerful sultan's palace guard in Baghdad as they were attempting to invade the sultan's harem one starry, moonlit night. The old sultan was roused from his slumbers and was in a foul mood when the three young men, stripped of their uniforms, were dragged before him in chains.

The sultan spat on each in turn and said, "Garbage! Filth! I spit on your balls! Blue-eyed devils try to fuck my wives, will you! After tonight you will no longer have pricks to fuck with! You'll have to squat to piss, and all men will know you have felt the wrath of the great Sultan of Baghdad!"

He kicked the first terrified Legionnaire in the head and said, "What did you do before you joined the Legion, camel dung?"

"I was a butcher," gasped the young man.

"Hack it off!" ordered the sultan to the captain of his guard. "And you, sheep twat?"

"I was a fireman," wailed the second Legionnaire.

"Oh, good!" cooed the sultan. "Burn it off!"

At this moment the third young Legionnaire, lying there naked in chains, began to laugh hysterically.

"Why are you laughing, vulture meat?" screamed the enraged sultan.

"Lollipops! I made lollipops!"

The Secret Code

"Ronnie, your fly's open," she said to her husband in the elevator.

"Oh, darn, Mommy, it keeps doing that."

"Well, we can't have you walking around the ambassador's reception with your pants unzipped."

"We can't, Mommy?"

"Of course we can't, dear. God only knows what the press would make of it, not to mention that smarmy ambassador with the gimlet eyes."

"Maybe I should go home."

"No, we can't do that either. The international repercussions might be bad for the country. If your zipper comes down, I'll whisper to you that your compact is open. That will be our secret code. Can you remember that, Ronnie?"

"I think so, Mommy. But what if my compact really is open?"

"Silly, you don't have a compact. Just remember if I whisper your compact is open, you should turn aside and zip up your fly."

Ronnie remembered and the secret code worked several times during the evening until, "Ronnie," whispered his wife, "have you been to the men's room?"

"Why, Mommy," he whispered back, "how did you know?"

"Because your compact's open," she hissed, "and your lipstick's hanging out!"

Set 'Em Up, Joe

The three vampires appeared in the shadows at the corner. They glided quickly and unseen up the street and into the bar. The bartender nodded to and addressed each in turn, "Ah, Count. Count. Count. What'll it be?"

"Joseph, dear friend," said the first. "I'd like something hearty and full-blooded, like the deep, ruby red of a fine burgundy."

"Good evening, Joseph," said the second. "Bring me something more delicate in shade, like an exquisite, light rosé. That would be nice."

"Just a cup of hot water, Joseph," said the third.

"A cup of hot water, Count? Aren't you feeling well?" asked Joseph.

"Not at all well," the count replied pulling out a used tampon. "I'll make tea!"

The Quality of Life

A cucumber, a dill pickle, and a penis were comparing what it means to be a cucumber, a dill pickle, and a penis.

The cucumber said: "Being a cucumber is really a lousy existence. They let me grow on the vine in the sunshine and breezes until I'm big and fat and juicy. And then they pick me, peel me, chop me up in a salad, and eat me."

The dill pickle said: "Well, I start out pretty much like you do. They let me grow and get big and fat and juicy, and then they pick me, drown me in a vat of vinegar and garlic and spices for a couple of months, and then they cut me up and eat me."

The penis said: "I admit you guys have it pretty rough, but listen to what happens to me. They let me grow and get big and fat and juicy, and then at two o'clock in the morning, they wake me up, put a plastic baggie over my head, shove me in a dark cave, and make me do pushups until I puke!"

Tattooed

"Really, Cecily, I never buy panties anymore. I have them tattooed on," said Linda to her friend.

"Tattooed?" asked Cecily in wonderment. "Tattooed? You've got to be kidding."

"Not at all, my dear. I found this crazy little tattoo artist who convinced me it was easy, cheap, and very efficient. And it drives Roger absolutely wild. All he can talk about is trying to fuck the pants off me. Only when we're alone, of course."

"Wasn't it painful?" asked Cecily.

"Fifteen dollars never to wash out undies in the sink again? No, it wasn't painful. Check it out, my dear. Here's his name and address, strictly confidential, by appointment only. Very smart, I wouldn't be surprised if it becomes the absolute rage."

Several weeks later, Cecily did check it out.

"No," she said to the crazy little tattoo artist, "I don't want panties. That's a little too-too, don't you think? But I was considering a skimpy little bra, perhaps. Something lacy in pale blue would be nice."

"Twenty-five bucks, kiddo," responded the crazy little tattoo artist.

"Twenty-five dollars? But you only charged my friend Linda fifteen dollars for panties."

"Yeah, but I had to go into the hole on that one."

"Well, couldn't you take a licking on this one?"

Invitation to a Royal Honeymoon

Saint Paul's Cathedral had never looked lovelier. The news wires were jumping with all the latest information and gossip about the royal wedding. London was jammed with tourists. Royal geegaws were selling by the crateload. Merry Old England had never been merrier than for the wedding of the Prince and Princess of Wales.

But on the first night of the royal honeymoon, it was an entirely different story when the prince and his new princess were finally behind closed doors, alone, and naked as commoners.

"I suppose it all does come down to this?" asked the princess shyly.

"Yes, I suppose it does. No, I mean, not if you're too tired. Do you have a headache?"

"No, my beloved, I'm yours. Take me."

And he proceeded to, with an inordinate artfulness for one who presumably had little practice. The prince was well nigh down the home stretch and champing at the bit to cross the finish line when the princess pushed him up from her enough to ask, gasping with delight, "Darling, darling . . . is this . . . ahhh . . ." she moaned, ". . . is this what the common people call fucking?"

"Yes!" responded the prince, panting to enter the winner's circle.

"Ah . . . ah . . . ah!" gasped the princess. "It's too good for them!"

Bwanabangi Love

King Bwanabangi of Tanzaswazi in Central Africa fell in love with a very proper and beautiful New England girl and proposed marriage. Unfortunately, the pure young New England girl spilled the beans to her society-matron mother, who threw a snit not to be believed.

"Indeed! Indeed, indeed, indeed! You can't be serious, Melinda. You must get rid of him at once. Ask him for something he can't possibly give you. I know, a diamond necklace! That ought to discourage the cheeky lout!"

Several days later Melinda came back with a stunning diamond necklace, the likes of which not even her mother could appraise at a single glance.

"You see, Mummy, he truly does love me. He said, 'When Bwanabangi is in love, money is no object!' "

"We'll just see about that," said her mother. "Ask the filthy beast for a deed and bill of sale for the *QE 2*. Jolly Old England will never let us down!"

Several days later Melinda came back with a deed and bill of sale in her name for the most luxurious ocean liner in the world.

"Mummy, he's so sweet. He said, 'When Bwanabangi is in love, he loves to give presents!' "

"All right, it's time to get dirty!" stormed Mummy. "Tell that jive turkey you simply couldn't consider marrying any man whose penis is less than sixteen inches long. Melinda, do you understand? P-E-N-I-S! You do know what a penis is, don't you? Then stop that stupid blushing and get on the phone!"

A few minutes later Melinda returned in tears, "Do you know what he said, Mummy? Do you? Do you?! He said . . . he said, 'When Bwanabangi is in love, Bwanabangi cuts it short!' "

Gladly, the Cross-eyed Bull

"Hello, Doc Fields? This is Farmer Prufrock. You better get out of here right away. Something's happened to my champeen bull, Gladly. Some durn fool left his pen gate open, and he charged the henhouse. I don't know why, probably 'cause of that Mozart music I was pipin' in to make the biddies lay. Anyway, he knocked himself colder than a mackerel, and now his eyes's so crossed he can't even walk."

The veterinarian drove out to the Prufrock place, and after examining Gladly, said, "Nothing to worry about, just run this piece of glass tube up his ass and blow on it real hard. Them eyes'll pop back just like new."

Farmer Prufrock greased up the glass tube and slid it up Gladly's rectum, leaned down, and blew as hard as he could.

"Anything?" he asked Doc Fields, who was holding Gladly by the ring in his nose.

"Not yet, better try it again."

Old Farmer Prufrock blew and blew until he couldn't see straight.

"Here, let me give it a try," said Doc Fields, pulling the glass tube out, turning it around, and running it back up the bull's rectum. He leaned over to blow, but Farmer Prufrock grabbed him.

"What the heck you doing, Doc?"

"Well, you don't think I'm gonna blow on the same end you did, do you?" asked the vet.

Respect

On the night of Cathy and Bob's fifth wedding anniversary, Cathy said to Bob, "You've been so good to me for the past five years. I couldn't have asked for a more kind, considerate husband. Is there anything special you want or would like me to do to show how much I love you?"

"Well, yes," replied Bob, "you've never put your mouth on my . . ." Bob hesitated. "You've never gone down, er, Cathy, I'd really like a blowjob."

"Oo, yuck, ptewy, ptewy," spat Cathy. "Oo, yuck, disgusting, how could you, oh, it's revolting, oo, ick." And she turned off the light and went to sleep.

On the nights of their tenth, fifteenth, and twentieth wedding anniversaries, Cathy had increasingly more praise for Bob and each time asked what would be his heart's delight. And each time he pleaded for oral love, which she refused emphatically.

And then on the night of their twenty-fifth wedding anniversary, Cathy said, "Bob, you've been such a good man to me all these years, and they've been good years, haven't they, Bob? Yes, they have. The best twenty-five years of my life. Bob, what can I do to show how much I love you? And don't start that disgusting crap about you-know-what!"

"Disgusting crap, disgusting crap? It's perfectly natural between a man and a woman, a married man and woman, a man and woman who've been married twenty-five years. Once, just once, so I can know what it's like before I die. Is that so much to ask?"

"Men go to whores for that sort of thing. If a wife does it, the husband doesn't respect her anymore."

"Cathy, I love you. I respect you. I've never even looked at another woman but you. Please, Cathy, just this once, please."

"Promise me that you'll still respect me in the morning if I . . . no, I don't think I could, no, I know I couldn't. But if I tried, Bob, if I tried and actually managed to do what you want, you promise me you'll still respect me in the morning?"

"Oh, Cathy, yes, yes, I could never lose my respect for you."

So Cathy gave him the much longed-for blowjob, then rushed off to the bathroom to spit, rinse, and gargle. The phone rang. Bob answered and called out to Cathy, "Hey, cocksucker, it's for you!"

Major Medical

"Doctor," said Mr. Currie, "I woke up this morning with this red ring around my penis. I've been to two doctors already today, and I'm really worried about it."

"Well, Mr. Currie," replied the doctor, "let's have a look-see." After examining the strangely afflicted organ, the doctor said, "I don't think there's too much to worry about, Mr. Currie, I can definitely get rid of the red ring around your penis."

"Oh, Doctor, you can? I can't tell you how relieved I am. How much will the treatments cost?"

"I'd say about twenty dollars for the office visit."

"Twenty dollars?" wondered Mr. Currie. "The first doctor I saw today said it would take at least one hundred eighty dollars' worth of treatments to remove it, and the second doctor said over three hundred dollars. How can you remove it for only twenty?"

The doctor smiled and replied, "Probably because those other two quacks just don't know lipstick when they see it!"

What It Is Is

"Now, class," said Miss Pimm reaching into her desk drawer out of sight of the first-graders, "I'm holding something in my hand that's round and has a bumpy surface. Who can tell me what it is?"

"Oo, oo, ah!" insisted Harry shooting his hand up in the air.

"Yes, Harry, what do you think it is?"

"A basketball!" said Harry.

"No, Harry, it's an orange," said Miss Pimm placing the orange on her desk, "but you're thinking, you're thinking. Now, class, I'm holding something in my hand that's flat and green. Who can tell me what it is?"

"Oo, oo, ah!" again Harry's hand shot up in the air.

"No one else has a guess? All right, Harry, what do you think it is?"

"A dead frog!" said Harry enthusiastically.

"No, Harry, it's a ten-dollar bill," said Miss Pimm, "but you're thinking, you're thinking."

"Miss Pimm?" asked Harry. "Can I try?"

"*May* I try," corrected Miss Pimm. "*May* I try."

"Yeah, sure. May I try, Miss Pimm?"

"Yes, Harry, you may try."

"Now, class," said Harry stuffing his hand into his pocket, "I'm holding something in my hand that's long and hard and has a red head on the end of it. Who can tell me what it is?"

"Harry!" said Miss Pimm, "I know what you've got in your hand, and I'll not have that kind of business in my classroom."

"No, Miss Pimm, it's a kitchen match," said Harry, "but you're thinking, you're thinking!"

Shore Leave

A navy man on shore leave struck up a conversation with a tarty-looking young thing at a sidewalk café and invited her to a nearby bar for a drink. Their bar conversation was rife with sexual innuendo and come-ons, so he asked her to take a walk down by the lake. When they reached a secluded section, he openly propositioned her.

"Say, what kind of girl do you think I am?" she asked haughtily.

"The kind of girl who got picked up by a sailor, let him buy her drinks, led him on, and walked all the way down here so she could lie down in the grass and get the best fuck she's ever had."

"My, my, my, aren't you the cocky one?" she sneered.

"That's right, prick-tease, I've got two cocks! That's why there's two sets of buttons on my pants."

"Put up or shut up, shark bait!"

So he unbuttoned the right set of buttons and pulled out the biggest piece of seafood she'd ever seen. The next thing she knew she was on her back in the grass, her knees pressed up against her shoulders, taking the old heave-ho like a pay-as-you-go girl.

After they were both spent and lying in a heap like Raggedy Ann and Andy, she said, "That was okay, but I bet you could do better with the other one."

"What?"

"Your other cock—you promised me two."

Dutifully, he disengaged, stuffed the first back into

his pants, buttoned up, unbuttoned the left set of buttons, and pulled out his "left" cock. But stroke, pet, slap, and nibble as she might, the "left" one didn't rise to the occasion.

"What a cheap trick you are," she said nastily. "What's the good of having two cocks if one of them doesn't work?"

"Take it easy, all right? Give him a chance. Nobody likes sloppy seconds!"

"362"

At the dirty-joke convention, those jokesters really know their dirty jokes. In fact they know them so well, they don't even bother telling them anymore. Each joke has a number assigned to it, and instead of telling the whole joke, they just tell them by number.

For example, Lewd Louie from Detroit stood up and told "186!" The conventioneers went hysterical, laughing, guffawing, and slapping each other on the back.

Filthy Fred from Dallas stood up and told "518!" What a riot of merriment filled the hall.

Suggestive Sal from Sacramento got up and told a really subtle "91!" And she got a standing ovation.

Then Mad Max from Miami Beach got up and told a boisterous "362!" A smattering of polite smiles, and then one rude "Ha-ha-ha" echoed throughout the hall.

"Shit!" said Mad Max as he sat down. "I never could get that one right!"

Salvation

It was time for Father Murphy's Saturday-night bath and young Sister Mary Michael had prepared the bath water and towels just the way the old nun had instructed. Sister Mary Michael also remembered just what her instructions were: not to look at Father Murphy's nakedness if she could help it, do whatever he instructed her to do, and pray.

The next morning the old nun asked Sister Mary Michael how the Saturday-night bath had gone.

"Oh, Sister," said the young nun dreamily. "I've been saved."

"Saved? And how did that fine thing come about?" asked the old nun.

"Well, when Father Murphy was soaking in the tub, he asked me to wash him, and while I was washing him the Lord guided my hand down between his legs where the Lord keeps the Key to Heaven."

"Did He now," said the old nun evenly.

"And Father Murphy said that if the Key to Heaven fit my lock, the portals of Heaven would be opened to me and I would be assured of salvation and eternal peace."

"Go on," said the old nun more evenly.

"And then Father Murphy guided his Key to Heaven into my lock."

"Is that a fact," said the old nun even more evenly.

"At first it hurt terribly, but Father Murphy said the pathway to salvation was often painful and that the glory of God would soon swell my heart with ecstasy. And it did, it felt so good being saved."

"The wicked old Devil," said the old nun. "He told me it was Gabriel's Horn, and I've been blowing it for forty years!"

The Bet

Jim and Charlie were jocking it up and getting drunk at the football game when Jim turned around and thought he saw a woman sitting about ten rows behind them with her legs spread open and black pubic hair showing deep between them. "Jesus, God, Charlie, get a load of that broad back there with her pussy hairs showing!"

Charlie craned around and focused on the woman. "You're a drunk mess of a skunk's asshole, Jim. Them ain't pussy hairs, them's black lace panties."

"Pussy hairs."

"Black lace panties."

"Pussy hairs!"

"Black lace panties!"

Well, they decided to wager a week's pay on their individual opinions and that Jim, since he had seen her first and was the one most likely to make it up to the beer concession and back, should do just that and get a closer look between the woman's legs as he passed. When he came back he sat down looking a little green around the gills.

"Well, did I win?" asked Charlie. "Is it black lace panties?"

"Nope."

"Oh, shit, you mean them's pussy hairs?"

"Nope."

"Well, if it ain't black lace panties and it ain't pussy hairs, what is it?"

"Flies."

The Greatest Thing in the World

Little Tommy and his playmate Joey were wondering when they would be able to get a penis, and then they couldn't make up their minds what color penis they would get, if they could get one.

"What color would you get?" asked Tommy.

"I don't know," answered Joey. "What's a penis?"

"You don't know?"

"No. Don't you?"

"No. I thought you did," said Tommy. "Wait here, I'll go ask my dad. He knows everything."

Tommy's dad answered, "Well, Tommy, a penis is . . . well, a penis, well. . . . Here, I guess the best way to explain a penis to you is to show you mine." With that he unzipped his fly, pulled out his penis, and held it in his hand.

"This is a penis, Tommy. Every man has one. When you grow up, you'll have one, too. Oh, you've got one now, only it's a little boy's penis. A man's penis, well, Tommy, a man's penis is just about the greatest thing in the world."

Tommy ran back to his little playmate Joey, and, following his father's example, said, "Well, Joey, the best way to explain a penis is to show you mine." And he unbuttoned his little fly, pulled out his penis, and held it in his hand.

"This is a penis, Joey," said Tommy proudly, "and if it gets to be a whole lot smaller like my dad's, it'll be the greatest thing in the world!"

The Mighty Dong

"The kid's magnificent!" raved his agent. "The Mighty Dong! Can't you see it on the marquee now? The Mighty Dong! Champion of Love! Fifty girls a night without missing a stroke! I'm telling you, Bruce, this is going to sell! We'll both be rich men, believe me. Twenty thousand a night and you provide the girls. Deal?"

"No way, José, five thousand a night and you supply the girls."

"Bruce. Brucey, baby, what can I say? You're like a son to me. Ten thousand a night and you supply the girls."

"It's a deal. But the girls are going to have to double up, wear wigs or something. I'm not paying fifty broads a night to do the work of one good whore. When can he start?"

"Saturday night."

The arena was crowded to capacity that Saturday night, and when The Mighty Dong dropped his robe and stood naked before the throng, a gasp of delight rose from the women and a groan of envy from the men.

"Well, he certainly lives up to his name," hissed one woman to her friend. "Now let's see if he can live up to his fame."

And the pageant began, but after the twenty-sixth girl, it suddenly came to an end. The Mighty Dong lay spent on the canvas, exhausted, gasping for air. The crowd went berserk, hooting, whistling, and demanding their money back.

"What're you trying to do, ruin me?" screamed his agent over the noise of the crowd. "Get up, you cruddy turd, and finish the job!"

"I don't understand it," wept the broken Dong. "It went so well at rehearsal this afternoon!"

To Tell the Truth

Goldie, Ruth, and Sarah were sitting around the pool of their condominium in Miami, drinking their first round of martinis for the afternoon and discussing the merits of their respective husbands.

Goldie said, "Oh, my Sol, he's such a good man. He loves me so much. Just to show me how much he loves me, he gave me this ring. You see this ring? A diamond. Six carats. Now I ask you, is that love or what?"

Ruth said, "Yes, and my Bernie, oh, how that man loves me. This coat, you see this coat I'm wearing already? Black sable. Did you ever? A full length Russian black sable coat. He's so good to me."

Then Sarah said, "Well, my Hymie, he's a fine man. Thoughtful, considerate, and when we make love, he finds me so exciting—when he's aroused, eleven pigeons can roost on his erect pishie."

After several more rounds of martinis, the ladies were feeling really relaxed and at peace with the world and each other.

Goldie said, "Girls, I'll tell you a little secret. My Sol, yes, he's a good man and he loves me like I was sixteen. But this ring? It's a zircon."

Ruth said, "Well, my Bernie's always worked hard and now we're retired and he said to me, 'Ruthie, you want a full-length coat of black sable, we can't afford it. Dyed rabbit we can afford.' He loves me so much, he cried when I said yes."

Then Sarah said, "Well, I guess I have a little confession to make, also. My Hymie, he really finds me terribly sexy, but you know, even when he gets fully aroused, that eleventh pigeon has to lean a little!"

Flying the Jolly Roger

After three months at sea, a young sailor can get as horny as an eight-point buck in rutting season. After nine months at sea a young sailor might mention to the first mate that if shore leave isn't coming pretty soon, the young sailor might leap right out of his mind.

"Now, listen, Young Jim, the sea is the great provider and can even provide for a man's physical needs in her infinite wisdom. Just go down to the forecastle hold and you'll find off to the left in a corner this barrel with the bunghole. When you think you just might pop out of your skull, go down there and stick your Jolly Roger through the hole."

The first mate's words were still hanging on the air when Young Jim hit the forecastle hold, his Jolly Roger ready in hand. He pushed it through the bunghole in the barrel and felt a warm pair of lips surround it.

Life at sea had never been better and Young Jim proved to be a capable and first-rate sailor. He made frequent use of the barrel with the bunghole in the forecastle hold and never missed an opportunity to thank the first mate for letting him in on this wonderful secret of the sea.

One evening Young Jim sauntered down to the forecastle hold looking for a bit of boldness with what he had come to believe was a barrel surely made in heaven just for him. He thrust his Jolly Roger through the bunghole, but nothing happened. He pushed his Jolly Roger in and out of the bunghole, but no sweet charity was to be found. He raced off to find the first mate and told him of this ill wind that had filled the ship's sails.

"Ah, my lad," shrugged the first mate wisely, "it must be your turn in the barrel."

Cherry Picker

Peddling encyclopedias in rural America isn't the life it's cracked up to be. It was sunset and Chip was hot and tired and dusty when he pulled up in front of the rambling, rundown farmhouse.

"Yep," said the farmer, "what you need is a wash, a good supper, and a sweet night's sleep in my haymow. What's that you got in the back seat of your car, encyclopedias? My, ain't they fancy. Tomorrow we can talk about them. Maybe one of my darlin' daughters needs a set."

Chip doubted it. All three of the farmer's daughters had the prettiest sets he'd ever seen. The girls washed him, fed him, and put him to bed. He was just dozing off when a shadowy figure climbed the ladder to the haymow and snuggled in beside him.

"I just knew you was a good man the first I laid eyes on you," said the oldest daughter as she guided his instantly erect penis into her. After they were both spent, she began to bawl and caterwaul and point to the sticky red stuff between her legs and said, "Oww, look what you gone and done. You busted my cherry, and I'm gonna tell my daddy, and he'll blow your head off with his shotgun unless you give me fifty dollars."

Chip paid her and lay there shaking, too dazed to doze, when the second daughter slipped in beside him and kissed, petted, and fondled until he couldn't control himself and screwed her royally. She, too, burst into tears and pointed to the sticky red stuff between her legs, "Lookie, lookie what you done, you busted my cherry and my daddy's gonna blow your head off unless you pay me fifty dollars."

Chip paid, she left, and he began to dress and gather his things to get out of there when the youngest daughter climbed on top of him. Even though he was frightened and tired, she was so young and sweet and soft that he stuck her before he could control himself and thought he was dying and going to heaven when he came. Then she immediately burst into tears and, pointing to her ravaged vagina, which was sticky green, she said, "Oh, my daddy's gonna kill you when he sees you've busted my cherry."

"Busted your cherry? Hey, what's going on here? Cherries aren't green."

"Oh, yeah?" she screamed. "Well, you gotta pay double for bustin' *my* cherry 'cause it ain't even ripe yet!"

Détente

"Hello, Mr. Secretary of State? It was good of you to accept my call. My name is Peter Burns of the Goodrich Rubber Company. What? Ah, yes, ha-ha-ha, I do get a lot of ribbing about my name. What? Ah, no, we're not the one with the blimp. That's the other one. No, I didn't call you about air space over the Rose Bowl. Well, you see, sir, we've received this order from the Soviet Union. Yes, sir, I mean Russia. They've placed an order for two million condoms. No, sir, not the kind with the little tickly knobs on the end, just the plain old prophylactic sheaths. And we don't want to ship two million rubbers to Russia without clearing it with you first, sir. You will? Thank you very much, sir. I'll wait for your memorandum."

Several days later the official memorandum from the State Department arrived.

"Order approved. Manufacture immediately two million condoms requested by Soviet Union. Specifications as follows: twelve inches long, four inches in diameter, stamped 'Size Medium—Made in the U.S.A.!'"

Modern Times

"Honey, surprise!"

"Eddie, what are you doing home so early?"

"You know what they say about operating heavy machinery with a hard-on."

"You left work early because of sex? Oh, Eddie, give me a break."

"Ah, honey, just because I'm crazy in love with you and can't even think about you without getting turned on?"

"Well, I'm not an electric switch you can 'turn on' any time you feel like it. If you're that sex crazed, see a whore every now and then."

"A whore? Are you nuts?"

"Edward, we're living in modern times. I'm just not in the mood right now. Is that so terrible? Think modern, go see a whore."

"You're nuts, Julie, nuttier than a fruitcake!"

And he slammed out of the apartment, barreled down the stairs, and ran smack into their downstairs neighbor, Karen.

"Hey, watch it, big guy, you should call signals when you're about to tackle the whole world."

He apologized. She recognized his anger, uncovered the reason, and invited him in to get it off his chest. She also gave him a trip around the world and a nut-wrenching lay he'd never forget.

When he got back upstairs, he said to Julie, "Thanks, honey. You may be nuts, but I can see your point of view. Modern times, you were too long in a coming!"

"Why? What do you mean?"

"I ran into Karen on my way out. I was so mad she invited me in to cool off, and, my little modern thinker, you could learn a few things from her on how to please your man. I gave her twenty bucks like you said, and I'm home, happy as can be."

"Twenty bucks!" screamed Julie. "Why that dirty whore, I never took a penny from her husband!"

Petey Want a Polly

Gerald's parrot, Petey, was so morose and indifferent that he couldn't even hold on to his perch and kept falling to the bottom of his cage. Gerald went to the pet shop seeking some solace for his disconsolate bird. The pet-shop owner hesitantly suggested that perhaps Petey just needed a good time with a suitable female parrot to give him back his *joie de vivre*. Being a respectable pet-shop owner and not a Polly-pimp, it was hard to convince him to loan Gerald one of his female birds for the night, so hard, in fact, that it cost Gerald fifty dollars.

Gerald took the female parrot home and put her in the cage with Petey. Petey cast a baleful eye on the exotic female and fell off his perch to lie beak-up on the floor of his cage.

"Listen, Petey," cajoled Gerald, "this lovely Polly just cost me fifty dollars for the night, so get off your well-feathered ass and at least make her welcome." With this he dropped the cloth over the cage and left the room. Soon after he heard such squawking and screeching that he ran into the room and tore the cover from the cage. There lay the female bird, help-less under Petey's savage attack, her feathers flying and her puckered underskin showing through in many places.

"Jesus, Petey, what are you doing?" yelled Gerald at his bird.

And Petey screamed back at him, gleefully ripping out more of her feathers, "For fifty bucks a night I want her naked, naked, naked!"

For Old Times' Sake

Lord Beaverdam was residing at his baronial seat in the country about eighty miles outside of London. Although in his younger days he'd been quite the roué, those days had long since passed when the delights of London night life held any interest for him.

One evening while soaking in his hot bath, playing with his rubber ducky, and watching the bubbles caused by his old-man farts rise to the surface and pop, something strange appeared—a bulbish, red, throbbing pole rose in the water before him. For a moment he was frightened, thinking it might be the periscope of a U-boat, but then something in the recesses of his memory clicked and he thought to himself, Good heavens, that's me, I've got an erection!

He immediately rang the little bell that summoned his loyal manservant. When Jeeves arrived, the old man was leaning back in the tub, chuckling with admiration for his refound treasure.

"Jeeves, look, Jeeves!" cried the delighted Lord Beaverdam. "I've got a hard-on!"

"So it would appear, your Lordship," said the less than enthused Jeeves. "And a mighty pole it is, too. Shall I call her Ladyship?"

"Not bloody likely," replied the cunning old man. "Bring me my baggiest pants. Maybe I can smuggle this one up to London!"

Mira, Mira!

Carmencita knocked gently on her mistress's bedroom door. As the new maid in an elegant home, she didn't want to disturb her mistress if she wasn't already awake. But receiving no reply, she quietly opened the door and entered the darkened bedroom. She opened the heavy drapes to let the sunshine in and saw something on the floor that caused her to scream in terror. The butler rushed from the pantry and found Carmencita sitting on the floor in a maelstrom of tears.

"My God, Carmencita, what on earth's the matter?"

"Mira, mira!" cried Carmencita pointing to the offending object on the floor.

"Oh, really, child, pull yourself together," chided the butler. "Don't you use those things in Puerto Rico?"

"Sí, Señor, sí!" sobbed Carmencita. "But we don't skin them!"

Miss New Jersey

"I've never made love to a real Miss New Jersey before," he said.

"You may not tonight, either," replied Miss New Jersey. "I'm very particular about my body and any man's idea of it. Being Miss New Jersey is a terrific responsibility, and I can relate every part of my body to a city in New Jersey. What would you think if I were to show you my breast?"

"I'd say your breast would be a very Point Pleasant indeed," he answered.

"You really know your Miss New Jersey, don't you? What if I were to show you my bottom? What would you think?"

"If I could see your bottom, it would be like a holiday in Asbury Park."

"That's very good, I'm beginning to like you more and more. And what if I'd let you caress my vagina?"

"If I could caress your vagina, I'd feel like I'd died and gone to Cherry Hill."

"Sorry, wrong number. I was thinking more of Eatontown!"

The Hitchhiker

On a little-traveled road in Texas, Brad was driving along one night, tired from a day trying to peddle books in a string of ditchwater towns. A man stepped onto the pavement ahead of him and flagged him down. Brad, being a decent soul, pulled over to the side and rolled down his window. The man jabbed a pistol in his nose.

"Out of the car, mister!"

"But, but, but . . ."

"I said get out of the car—now move it!"

Brad got out slowly, sweat trickling down his neck, the feel of cold steel against his nose.

"Now jerk yourself off!" ordered the gunman.

"But, but, but . . ."

"How'd you like to breathe through three holes in your nose instead of two, mister? Now jerk!"

Brad did as he was told, taking longer than usual due to the stress of the circumstances.

"That's fine, mister, now do it again!"

"But, but, but . . ."

"Again!"

Poor Brad pulled and yanked and stroked and again managed to obey the command.

"Once more, and hurry it up! I don't have all night!"

"You don't have. . . !"

Brad heard the cock of the gun and out of the corner of his eye could see the gunman began to squeeze the trigger. He began flailing his poor, dead dick furiously, pleading, "All right, all right!"

Finally, finally he managed to expel a minuscule drop of pearly liquid and collapsed against his car, oblivious to the gun's threat. At this moment a lovely girl stepped from the bushes, and the gunman, all smiles, helped Brad to his feet.

"Gee, mister," said the gunman. "I'd be awful grateful if you'd give my sister a lift in to Abilene!"

Congratulations!

"Howie, hey man, I heard you got married!"

"Yeah . . . yeah . . . I got married."

"What a surprise, you sly fox you, I never had you picked as the type to settle down in a snug harbor."

"Yeah . . . well . . . I got married."

"Hey, why so glum, chum? How'd it go? The wedding night, I mean. Howie, what's the matter? Howie, stop that crying! Man, what happened? Here, take my handkerchief."

"What a disaster. What a disaster!"

"What happened, Howie, did you have trouble, you know, performing? I understand that can happen, nerves, that kind of thing."

"Oh, no, I was fantastic, the best ever. God, I could have gone on all night, almost did. And she's the greatest, the absolute greatest, I can't believe how talented that lady is. In fact she was so great that night, the next morning I left a fifty-dollar bill on her dressing table out of force of habit."

"Uh-oh, that must have got you in the dog house."

"No, no, that's just it! She was still half asleep, too, and gave me thirty bucks in change!"

The Ultimate Dream

Bart loved cunnilingus. His ultimate dream was to bury his face in the largest vagina he could find and never come up for air. Through some friends at the frat house, he had finally wangled a date with Bonnie

Lee Barnes, the coed on campus with a reputation for three-inch lips, labia minora, that is. Bart had quite a reputation of his own for having a six-and-a-half-inch tongue. They seemed made for each other.

Their big date could have sold tickets at scalpers' prices all over campus, but as it was they took a drive out to Spoon River in Bart's hatchback. They spread a blanket under the stars and before long were both naked and wrapped in each other's arms. He French-kissed dear Bonnie Lee until she almost gagged on that wondrous tongue, so he moved to her ear, her throat, then began the luxurious journey down her lovely body until he was face level with her crotch and its glorious bush of tawny blond hair. He circled her bush with his six-and-a-half-inch tongue, breathing in the musky dampness of her moistening vagina, then began the incredible journey into her. As he probed deeper and deeper, he had the sensation of sinking into furry, aromatic quicksand. His face was wet with her juices and his nose filled with the aroma of aroused pussy. He could faintly hear her sobbing with excitement when he felt her three-inch lips sucking on his ears and a muscular spasm from her vagina and the sensation of being sucked inside.

He landed with a soft *splut* and was surrounded by darkness. No Bonnie Lee Barnes, no blanket, no stars, only darkness.

"What the fuck?" he questioned the darkness.

"Bart!" answered a voice out of the darkness.

"Carl?! What happened? Where am I?"

"Never mind the questions now, kiddo. Just help me find my car keys, and I'll drive us both out of here!"

The Jinni in the Lamp

Shuffling through the sand at Brighton Beach, Bubba uncovered a beat-up old tin oil lamp. He picked it up and brushed it off to see if it might be worth the price of a hotdog when there was a flash of light, a puff of smoke, and the smell of bitter lemons. All this peculiar display lasted only a fraction of a second and wasn't noticed by anyone but Bubba and presumably the little ugly female in the tacky harem costume who now stood before him.

"So, what do you want?" asked the seedy little person.

"Huh?" counterqueried Bubba.

"Say, are you a wise guy or something? I'm the jinni in the lamp. You rubbed me the right way, and now I got to rub you back."

"Huh?" Bubba parried.

"Listen, are you stupid, or what? You rubbed the magic lamp. I'm the jinni who lives inside. I pop out. Surprise! Right? Now you get two wishes, so what'll it be? Gold, money, girls, what?"

"What do you mean, two wishes? I'm supposed to get three wishes."

"So now you're on the supreme court, already. A minute ago all you could say was 'Huh?' and now you want to haggle. Listen, don't get greedy, take the two wishes, believe me."

"All right, all right. I want to be white, and I want to be surrounded by pussy."

"You got it bro'," and with a grinding bump of her pelvis, she said, "Presto! You're a tampon!"

45

Cock-a-doodle-doo

Farmer Prufrock's cock was a champion. He hated to leave it alone the night before the statewide farm exposition in which it was sure to win first prize. But Farmer Prufrock also hated to miss the latest Rita Hayworth movie that only had one night left to play at the Rialto Bijou downtown. So he hid his cock in the front of his farmer overalls and took it with him to the movies. He entered the theater just as the credits were rolling, found an empty seat near the back, sat down, opened the buttons of his fly, and pulled the head of his cock through the fly so it could breathe. By the time his eyes adjusted to the darkened theater, he was totally engrossed in the movie.

Pamela and Gwendolyn, the reigning old-maid sisters in town, were also enjoying the movie until Pamela nudged Gwendolyn and whispered, "Gwendolyn, I don't want you to get upset, but Farmer Prufrock is sitting next to me, and he's undone his pants and his, his thing is out."

"His thing?" whispered back Gwendolyn.

"You know, his thing!"

"Oh, you mean his thing. Well, haven't you ever seen a man's thing before?"

"Well, really, yes, of course I have."

"Then just ignore it."

"But I can't, this one keeps eating my popcorn!"

The Peach

Jim and Charlie were at a fruit stand, and Jim spotted some peaches he thought looked really nice, so he bought one. He took a bite and said, "My God, Charlie, this peach is delicious. This is the best-tasting peach a man ever put a pair of lips around. It tastes just like pussy."

46

"Pussy?" said Charlie. "No way, good buddy, your CB must have short-circuited, a peach can't taste like pussy."

"It sure as hell does," said Jim. "This peach tastes just like pussy, honest injun, swear-on-a-stack-of-Bibles pussy. Here, take a bite." And he handed over the peach to Charlie.

Charlie took a big bite, barely tasted it, and spat it out. "Jesus, this is awful! It's the worst peach I've ever tasted. It tastes just like shit!"

"Turn it around, stupid!" said Jim.

Beans, Beans, the Musical Fruit

Being shipwrecked on a desert island with nothing but a few palm trees and crates and crates of canned beans for several months can drive a man insane, so Len and Harry were pleased as punch one sunbaked afternoon when a plank drifted ashore with another human being clinging to it lifelessly.

The young sailor named Jim was alive and quickly revived with a drink of fresh water collected in empty bean cans and some of the protein-packed beans themselves.

That evening, huddling around the small fire they managed to make from driftwood collected and carefully dried out, they repasted on beans à la seaweed and were lazily fantasizing about life back home. Their imaginings were punctuated by the frequent passing of wind caused by the beans. First Len breezed out a prolonged, almost silent, certainly deadly, rush of air. Then Harry passed a relaxed zephyr in a fragrant whoosh. Then young sailor Jim let go with a machine-gun volley of staccato farts that should have been heard on the mainland.

Len jumped to his feet overjoyed. "Listen to that, Harry, we landed ourselves a virgin!"

Marriage, Italian Style

"Angelina, *bambina mia,* how beautiful you look for your wedding."

"Thank you, Mama."

"Angelina, my darling little girl, tonight, after the wedding when you and Tony are alone together, he's going to want to do things with you that a husband wants to do with his wife. Do you understand what I mean?"

"No, Mama."

"Ah, such purity, such innocence. To think it will end tonight. Don't worry, my beautiful baby girl, Tony is a gentle man, and how fortunate your beautiful new apartment is only two flights up from Papa and me. If Tony frightens you, just come down to me, no matter how late it is."

Later that night, after a truly lovely wedding and reception, Angelina's mama sat in her kitchen dreaming about her own wedding night when Angelina burst in, "Oh, Mama, I'm so afraid, Tony's awful, he's like an animal!"

"Shhhh, hush, *bambina,* tell Mama what happened."

"He took off his shirt and he's so hairy. He's got thick black hair all over his chest."

"Baby, baby, baby, that's nothing, many men are hairy like that. Now go back upstairs to your husband."

A little later Angelina again rushed into her mama's kitchen. "Oh, Mama, I'm going to kill myself, I don't understand. He took off his pants, and his legs are all hairy like a gorilla's. Oh, Mama, I'm going to die, I just know it."

"My angel, my treasure, that's nothing to be afraid of. All men have hairy legs, why, look at your brother, Frankie, he has hairy legs. Now, go back upstairs and be nice to Tony."

Again Angelina rushed in to her mother. "I can't, I can't stay up there, I'll die for sure, it's awful, please don't make me."

"Sweetheart, heart of my heart, what now?"

"He took off his underwear, Mama, and he has another foot between his legs."

"Another foot?"

"I couldn't look at it, I just couldn't, but I'm sure at least another foot."

"Angelina, *bambina mia*, that's different. You stay here, I'll go up."

The Good Old Days

After encountering that nasty Big Bad Wolf in the woods, Little Red Riding Hood was relieved to reach her grandmother's cottage. The shades were drawn and the cottage was dimly lit, but Little Red Riding Hood was happy to have reached its safety.

"Good afternoon, Grandmother," said Little Red Riding Hood, "I've brought you some honey and cakes."

"Bless you, my child," said her grandmother. "Put them on the table and come closer so I can give you a kiss."

Little Red Riding Hood did as her grandmother asked, but as she approached the old lady's bed, she hesitated.

"Why, Grandmother, what big ears you have."

"Better to hear you with, my child," replied her grandmother.

"Why, Grandmother, what big eyes you have."

"Better to see you with, my child," replied her grandmother.

"Why, Grandmother, what big teeth you have."

"Better to eat you with, my child," said the Big Bad Wolf, leaping out of bed and ripping off his grandmother disguise.

"Eat, eat, eat," snapped Little Red Riding Hood. "Doesn't anybody fuck anymore?!"

Promises, Promises

"Oh, Johnny, I've never been in a motel like this before. Look! A round water bed!" she giggled, falling backward onto the bed, "and mirrors on the ceiling! What a naughty place this is. What are you doing?"

Having kicked off his shoes, and pulling off his socks, "Getting undressed."

"Oh, Johnny, strip for me, like I saw on TV. Come on, Johnny, take it off."

Pulling down his pants and shorts in one gesture, "*Voilà!* Why are you screaming? Natalie, stop that screaming!"

"Oh, no you don't, you're not going to stick that big thing in me! What are you, some kind of freak!? Help! Stop!"

Clamping his hand over her mouth and trying to control her, "Natalie, listen to me. Natalie! I'm not going to hurt you, Natalie, would you stop and listen for a minute. I'll be gentle. I'll put one hand around the base and the other hand right over that, so you only have to take as much as you want. Okay? Natalie? Oh, God, Natalie, don't pass out on me. I won't hurt you."

"It's too big, Johnny, how did it get so big? You promise to keep both hands on it? Oh, it's so big. You promise?"

With that he rolled over on his back and put both hands on his monster hang. "I promise."

Pulling off her panties and straddling him, "I don't think I can, Johnny, I don't think I . . ." And she slid down on his shaft, and of course he removed his hands, allowing total entry.

After several moments of telling probing, she was glistening with perspiration and whispered, "Johnny . . . you could take away *one* of your hands now."

Inflatable Love

A whorehouse is to a sailor like honey is to a fly, and Captain Dan was a salty old salt with a three-month hard-on and a snoot full of rum. He wasn't exactly lay-down-dead drunk; he could still crawl when he got to the brothel and demanded the prettiest wench in the place.

All the girls were occupied, but the madam figured as drunk as old Dan was, Suzie, the Inflatable Goddess of Love, would keep him happy. So she half dragged, carried, and crawled old Dan up to the room where Suzie was waiting, all pumped up and eager for love. Captain Dan swore she was the prettiest little thing he had ever laid eyes on, so the madam left him happily trying to coax Suzie to go around the world with him.

Some time later a pitiful, agonized wail was heard from Suzie's room. The madam rushed in and found Captain Dan sitting on the bed naked as a jaybird sobbing, "I killed her, I killed her."

The madam sat with her arms around him, "Take it easy, Captain, take it easy, tell old Madam Helene what happened."

"I don't know what happened," sobbed Captain Dan. "We was having a wunnerful time, a wunnerful time. Then I bit her on the ass, she let a fart and flew out the window!"

The Baldheaded Mousie

Fifteen-year-old Billy was babysitting with his five-year-old sister, Debbie, and asked her if she'd like to see his baldheaded mousie.

"Yes, I guess so," doubted Debbie.

Billy unbuttoned his jeans and slowly pulled out his little baldheaded mousie.

"Gee, Billy, this doesn't look like a mousie to me," said Debbie. As she cupped the limp little creature in her hand, it gave a little pulsing throb. "Oh, look, Billy, he moved," said Debbie delightedly.

"That's not all he does," said Billy. "If you pet him and give him little kisses, he'll grow a lot bigger and stronger," coaxed Billy. Debbie petted her new little friend, and he gave some more of those little pulsing throbs and began to grow somewhat.

"Look, Billy, he likes me," said Debbie. "He's growing just like you said he would."

"Yes, I know," sighed Billy. "If you want him to grow really big, give him a few little kisses . . . please." And she did.

Several minutes later, Debbie and Billy's mother returned from the grocery store, heard a horrendous yell from her son, dropped her groceries, and rushed inside. Billy was nowhere to be seen, but Debbie was sitting on the living-room floor in tears.

"Debbie, baby, what happened? Where's Billy? Shhh, baby, it's all right, tell Mommy what happened."

Debbie could barely get her story out with her little-girl sobs and tears. Billy had let her play with his little baldheaded mousie. First she just held it, it was so cute. Then she petted it and it began to grow, so she gave it little kisses like Billy asked her to do, and then it really grew and got very hard and looked angry, but Billy said it was feeling just great.

"And then, Mommy," sobbed Debbie, "it spit all over my face, so I bit its little head off!"

The Pearly Gates

Three nuns were met by Saint Peter at Heaven's Pearly Gates. Each had to answer one question correctly to enter. The first nun approached Saint Peter and he asked, "Who was the first human being created by God?"

"Oh, that's an easy one," murmured the nun. "Adam." And the Heavenly Choir sang forth, the Pearly Gates swung open, and Saint Peter ushered her in.

"And what did God create from Adam's rib?" Saint Peter asked the second nun.

"Oh, that's an easy one," murmured the nun. "Eve." And the Heavenly Choir sang forth, the Pearly Gates swung open, and Saint Peter ushered her in.

"And what were the first words spoken to Adam by Eve?" Saint Peter asked the third nun.

"Oh, that's a hard one," murmured the nun. And the Heavenly Choir sang forth, the Pearly Gates swung open, and Saint Peter ushered her in.

The Red Ferrari

The mint-condition red Ferrari idled sensuously at the intersection, waiting for the light to change, when the speeding delivery truck changing lanes swerved into the Ferrari, and screeching to a stop, gave the occupants a jolt.

"Oh, my God. Oh, my God!" was all George could say as Al jumped out of the passenger side and raced around the front of their brand-new Ferrari. There in front of the driver's door was a three-inch gouge in the lustrous red finish. Al ran around to the truck driver and yelled, "What do you think you're doing? That car just came from the showroom and now it's ruined!"

"Ah, I just nicked it," growled the burly driver, climbing out of his truck.

"Nicked it? Nicked it? A three-inch gouge in a fifty-two-thousand-dollar Ferrari is not just a nick. It's a disaster! Show me your registration. I want your driver's-license number. Are you insured?" demanded Al.

"Ah, it's just a scratch," said the driver glaring down at the marred Ferrari. "Get off my back, will ya?"

"What do you mean? Get off your back!" shouted Al in disbelief as the truck driver climbed back into his cab. "George, be sure to get his license-plate number if he tries to leave the scene of the accident!" called Al to his friend.

The driver started his truck, but Al yanked the cab door open. "You're not going to get away with this. I'll sue. I'll take you to court so fast it'll make your head spin. We've got your license-plate number, it can be traced!"

"Ah, kiss my hairy asshole!" shouted the driver as he tried to close his door.

"George!" yelled Al to his friend, "what'll I do now? I think he wants to settle out of court!"

Good News, Bad News

"Well, Mr. Wilkens," said the doctor. "I have good news and bad news for you. Which would you like first?"

"You might as well give me the bad news first. That's how they always do it on Johnny Carson."

"The bad news, Mr. Wilkens—I want to be straight out front with you, Mr. Wilkens. You've only got six months to live."

"Six months?" said Mr. Wilkens paling visibly. "Only six months?"

"Yes, I'm very sorry, Mr. Wilkens. But! Don't forget the good news."

"The good news?" asked Mr. Wilkens weakly.

"Yes, the good news, Mr. Wilkens," said the doctor expansively. "Did you happen to notice my receptionist, Miss Fuchs? The gorgeous one, the girl with the jet-black mane of jungle-madness hair, the girl with the dark, almond-shaped eyes and the sweetest pair of melons that ever hung from the female form. She's the receptionist who's always so kind to you and interested in how you are, and her uniform is always unbuttoned just enough so you can see down between her sweet titties, and you can't seem to stop your tongue from licking your lips just a little. Do you remember her, Mr. Wilkens?"

"Yes, yes, yes I do," said Mr. Wilkens, momentarily forgetting his misery.

"Fine, Mr. Wilkens, fine, because the good news is I'm going to fuck her tonight!"

Honeymoon Express

In the heyday of train travel, John and Mo planned to honeymoon on the *Santa Fe Chief* from coast to coast. But somehow their reservations got mixed up, and instead of a sleeping compartment, the sassy young newlyweds got upper berths on opposite sides of the aisle. Eager to consummate their marriage, they worked out the plan that Mo would ask John to pass the grapefruit whenever the urge struck throughout the night, and he would hop across the aisle to her berth.

Not three seconds after the lights went out, Mo whispered, "Oh, Johnny, pass me the grapefruit."

And John hopped across the aisle into his beloved's eager waiting embrace. About three o'clock in the morning, for the fifth time, Mo ardently whispered, "Johnny, pass me the grapefruit."

And from the berth below Mo's came an angry voice.

"All right, enough's enough! Eat bananas instead —they don't drip!"

Naughtie Nightie

"I don't know what it is," Marilyn complained to the marriage counselor. "Ted just doesn't seem interested in me sexually anymore. We always had a good sex life, but lately . . . We've only been married three years, I've certainly kept my figure . . . I just don't understand it."

"Well, maybe it's something quite simple," offered the counselor. "Tell me, what's your nightly routine before you go to bed?"

"I generally go to the bathroom, do my toilette, and slip into my nightie," said Marilyn.

"Describe your nightie to me," said the counselor.

"It's pink. Ted always loves me in pink. It's cut very low in the back and high in the front," said Marilyn.

"Tonight, why don't you try something a little different. Break up the routine. It may be just the stimulus your husband needs to notice you again. Try wearing your nightie backward so it's cut high in the back and very low in the front. That ought to get his attention," suggested the counselor.

"Do you really think so?" thrilled Marilyn.

"Yes, it might just do the trick," assured the counselor.

So that night Marilyn went to the bathroom, did her toilette, and put on her nightie backward. She came out of the bathroom, shoulders back and points held high, and undulated across the room in front of her husband. Ted continued untying his shoelaces with no more than a glance at her. Marilyn undulated back across the room in front of him, this time humming a few bars from "Stranger in Paradise." Still no reaction from Ted.

"Ted," asked Marilyn seductively holding her hands behind her back and really pushing her perky

61

points up high, "don't you notice something different tonight?"

Ted looked up and said, "Yeah, you got shit on the front of your nightgown for a change!"

The Farmer's Daughter

"Look, Papa, up ahead, highwaymen!"

"Quick, daughter, climb into the back of the wagon. Take these gold coins and hide them so they won't be found."

And just in the nick of time, too, as the highwaymen descended on the hapless farmer, knocking him from the wagon and stripping him of his valuables. Then they dragged the poor girl from the wagon, searched her, and punched her to the ground.

"Pity!" cried the farmer. "Have pity on a poor farmer and his pox-ridden daughter!"

"Pox?!" yelped the filthy highwayman, who was about to skewer the poor girl with his smelly sirloin. "Let's get out of here!"

So the highwaymen piled onto the wagon and drove away, leaving the farmer and his daughter lying in the ditch.

"Well, lass, did they get the gold coins?"

"No, Father," said the tearful young girl.

"Hush, my child, dry your tears. You're a clever lass and a good daughter. Where did you hide them?"

"Oh, Father," blushed the girl, "between my legs inside me."

"Lordy, lordy," mused the farmer. "Too bad your mother wasn't here, we could have saved the horse and wagon, too!"

The Riddle

"Here's a riddle for you, Alan. A bank executive is interviewing three women for a very high-level job at the bank. The final question of the interview put to each candidate is, 'If you could steal two million dollars from the bank with absolutely no way of being caught, what would you do?'

"The first woman replied, 'In all honesty, my answer is I would take the two million.'

"The second woman answered, 'No, I couldn't take all that money, but I might take just a little bit of it; perhaps a hundred thousand or so.'

"The third woman said, 'No, no way would I touch a penny of that money. I just couldn't live with myself; after all, it's not my money. It would be dishonest.'

"So, Alan, the riddle is which of the three female candidates did the bank executive hire?"

"Well, it's not really a riddle at all, and the answer is fairly obvious. He hired the one who wouldn't steal the money."

"Nope, he hired the one with the biggest tits!"

Snakebite

Jim and Charlie set up their hunting blind a couple of miles south of town near a woods trail where the deer were known to pass. After several hours nipping on a quart of moonshine, Charlie stepped out of the blind to air his hog. He was caught midstream when the rattler struck. With a howl of pain and rage, he staggered back into the blind and collapsed.

"Rattler got me," said Charlie, head lolling and eyes rolling in fear.

"A rattler! Christ's sake, Charlie, where'd he get you?"

"My pecker!" wailed Charlie, "right on the head of my pecker!"

"You just lay there calm like, and I'll run to town and get Doc Friendly out here soon as I can."

Jim raced the couple of miles into town, but Doc Friendly was busy cauterizing Danny Beazley's fresh stump where the power saw had jumped him.

"What'll I do, Doc?" asked Jim. "Charlie's got bit by a rattler."

"Where'd it get him?"

"On the head of his pecker!"

"Hot damn!" said the Doc. "You better get back there fast and tie a tourniquet around it, cut an X where the fangs went in, and suck out that poison."

"Say what?"

"You got to suck out that poison or Charlie'll die."

Jim made it back to Charlie as fast as he could.

"Where's the Doc?" said Charlie.

"He ain't coming."

"Well, what'd he say?" moaned Charlie.

"Sorry, Charlie, he said you're gonna die!"

Slumber Party

Little Tommy's friend Joey was spending the night with him. Tommy's mother put them to bed at the usual hour, but they hid under the covers with a flashlight, looking at their toes; then they got into a pillow fight, but when Tommy pitched his football through the window trying to bean Joey, that was the last straw. Tommy's father tacked an old sheet over the window, and "lights out" meant "lights out." Ah, boys will be boys, and they fell asleep snuggled against each other.

But several hours later Joey woke Tommy up.

"Pssst, Tommy. Pssst! Wake up, I'm scared."

"Hmmm . . . wha . . . ?"

"Tommy, wake up. I hear something."

"Wha . . . what?"

"I hear something. I think it's a bear!"

"A bear?"

Little Tommy was wide awake, and he, too, heard something. Only it didn't sound like a bear, it sounded like his mother, moaning and crying.

They tiptoed down the hall to his parents' room. Tommy peeked through the keyhole, and there, in full view, were his naked mother and father engaged in very passionate lovemaking.

"What is it?" whispered Joey.

"I don't know," whispered Tommy, giving up his spot at the keyhole so Joey could look.

"Wow-eee!" giggled Joey. Tommy clamped his hand over Joey's mouth and dragged him back to the safety of his bedroom.

"They're weird," said Joey. "You think he was hurting her?"

"I don't think so," answered Tommy, a little woebegone.

"What's the matter?"

"Nothin'."

"Yes, there is. You gonna cry?"

"Nah."

"Then what's the matter?"

"Well, how come they get so mad if I just pick my nose?!"

The Golf Widow

Estelle was sick of being left alone each weekend while her husband went out and played golf, so she decided to find a golf pro and take some lessons on her own. Her first lesson was a little dismal—she just didn't seem to have the knack.

The golf pro told her, "Listen, Estelle, your swing is pretty good and you have a fair eye, but your grip on the club is too tense. You've got to hold the club gently and make it an extension of your body. Go home and practice. Hold the club as if it were your husband's penis."

Estelle dutifully did as she was told and at her next week's lesson was doing much better. After the lesson the golf pro told her, "You see what I told you? You've really improved. Now if you take the club out of your mouth, you can add fifty yards to your drive!"

Beauty and the Beast

It was on the third night of their big-game safari that Cecily was dragged from their tent by a gorilla. Three days later, after being raped, sodomized, brutalized, and generally given a hard time by the gorilla, Cecily was rescued. It was questionable for several months whether she would recover from the shock and savagery of her abduction and attack. But time heals all wounds, so they say, and Cecily gradually recovered to her former self.

Having lunch at Sardi's with her friend Linda, she burst into tears over her fruit cocktail.

"My dear, what is it?" asked her concerned friend. "Is there something wrong with your fruit cocktail?"

"No, no, it's fine," sobbed Cecily. "It just reminds me of . . . of . . . well, it just reminds me of what happened on safari."

"Cecily, Cecily, Cecily," said Linda. "That's behind you, you must put it out of your mind. It happened months ago and thousands of miles away. You mustn't be concerned with that gorilla now."

"But he hasn't written, he hasn't called!" sobbed Cecily.

The Test

Maurice was determined to marry a virgin. After the computer dating service failed him, his only contacts with the opposite sex came from singles' ads in neighborhood "buy and swap" papers. How could he meet a virgin; and once met, how could he be sure she was a virgin? Maurice devised a test. If he did find a young woman who met his personal taste and attractiveness standards, and if she seemed innocent and chaste, and if after several months of decorous dating she still hadn't displayed any behavior other than the most upright and virtuous, he would simply unzip his fly, pull out his member, and ask her if she knew what it was. If she recognized it as a male's penis, she failed.

At last, after many months of dating young women with questionable morals and lowering his personal taste and attractiveness standards, he found the young woman of his dreams. His meager advances were met with kind but firm rejection, she would only see G-rated movies, and she never allowed him more than a peck on the cheek when he left her at her door. He was in heaven.

After a fun-filled evening at the bowling alley, Maurice parked in front of her house. "Gloria," he said, "I guess you must realize that I'm very fond of you. In fact I'm much more than fond of you, Gloria. I have a very important question to ask you."

"Yes, Maurice," encouraged Gloria.

Maurice unzipped his fly and pulled out his member, "Have you ever seen anything like this before, Gloria?"

Gloria studied it a moment and replied, "No, Maurice, I can't say that I have."

"Gloria," said Maurice, not releasing his suspicions too easily, "it's a man's penis."

"What man?" asked Gloria.

"This man, me, Gloria, it's mine. It's my penis!"

"You're kidding."

"A man's penis, Gloria," with love swelling at the rout of suspicion, "a man's penis!"

"Oh, no."

"Oh, yes!" shot Maurice. "It's a cock, a dick, a ying-yang! Oh, Gloria!"

"Oh, come off it, Maurice, be real," said Gloria. "Ying-yangs are about ten inches long and black!"

The Gambler

Harry's father finally resorted to asking Miss Pimm to help break Harry's dreadful gambling habit. Miss Pimm accepted the challenge thinking that if she could make Harry lose just one bet, he might be cured. Also, she might be able to handle this one bleak spot in her second-grade class and actually teach Harry something. Her opportunity came that very afternoon when she kept Harry after school for farting in class. Harry was behind her at the blackboard writing "I will not make rude noises in class" one hundred times when suddenly he stopped and sniffed loudly.

"What is it, Harry?" asked Miss Pimm.

"Something smells funny. Bet you're having your period, huh, Miss Pimm?"

"Harry, I most certainly am not."

"Betcha fifty cents you are."

Seizing this golden moment to cure Harry of his gambling, Miss Pimm accepted the bet. And though not a living soul but her mother and her gynecologist had ever seen her naked, she swallowed her modesty, hefted her skirts, dropped her panties, and won the bet.

She sent Harry home and called his father. Blushing crimson, she managed to tell Harry's father of her victory and how she had cured Harry of his gambling.

"Cured, hell!" shouted Harry's father into the phone. "Just this morning he bet me five dollars he'd see your cunt by sundown!"

The Americans Are Coming,
the Americans Are Coming

What with jet lag, business appointments, a two-mar-
tini lunch, more appointments, drinks and dinner
with prospective clients, drinks at a local pub, and a
nightcap at the hotel bar, Jack and J.P. were sloshed
to the nines when they stumbled into their room at
the posh London hotel. There didn't seem to be any
sensible thing to do at that wee hour but fill paper
bags with water and hurl them from the seventeenth-
story window. After a disheveled search for paper
bags in their room, the bathroom, and closet, J.P.
opened the door to the adjoining room and stood
trying to focus on the naked woman lying on the bed.
As cavalierly as possible he said, "Whoops, tiddley-
tiddley, woo-woo," and backed out of the room, clos-
ing the door behind him.

"No kidding now," said J.P., "there's a naked lady
in there."

"Sounds pretty good to me. Let me take a peek
through the keyhole. Oh, shit, I'm going in there and
fuck her. Ooo-eeee, she's a hot one!"

"Has she moved?" asked J.P.

"I can't tell, the room's spinning too fast," answered
Jack as he opened the door and walked in on his
knees.

About twenty minutes later the adjoining door
opened and Jack, tripping on his dangling pants, fell
head-first back into the room.

"Psst, Jack, did you fuck her? Jack? Oh, hey, Jack,
yoohoo, oh, Jackass, did you fuck the pretty lady in
the next room?"

"Best damn fuck I ever had," said Jack. Then he
passed out.

"Me too, me too," said J.P. Struggling at his clothes,
he stumbled over Jack into the adjoining room and
closed the door. Within twenty seconds J.P. was back

and trying to drag Jack to his feet.

"Jesus, Jack, how could you do it? How could you fuck that poor naked lady in there? She's dead!"

"Dead? Oh my God, I thought she was just English!"

Blind Date

"What do you mean your blind date was with Steven last night?!"

"Listen, Gretchen dear, don't get your ass in an uproar. I didn't arrange it, he did."

"But, Betsy, he's my boyfriend."

"Not anymore, dear. I think he'll be putting his shoes under my bed from now on."

"I don't believe it! I just don't believe you could do this to me. You know how crazy I am about Steven. I ... we ... I even went all the way with him. He's the only one I've ever gone all the way with."

"Well, you're not the only one he's ever gone all the way with, not after last night, anyway."

"I can't believe it. I hate you, Betsy! How could you do this to me?"

"Oh, grow up, sweet Gretchen, I didn't do anything. Steven did it, and very well, I might add. Why don't you go yell at him?"

"But I love him. I don't believe you. He couldn't have. Not with you. He said he loved me."

"Well, what about that little tattoo?"

"You rat, you bitch, you rat-bitch! You even know about his tattoo?"

"Yes, indeed-ee, right there on his fat prick, tattooed in capital letters ... S-O-S."

"S-O-S? S-O-S?! Well, he may have gone to bed with you, but he didn't go all the way. Because when he goes all the way, Betsy, sweetheart, rat-bitch, that tattoo on his fat prick doesn't spell S-O-S, it spells SOUVENIR OF SASKATCHEWAN!!!"

A Myth Is as Good as a Mile

The president of the United States and the ambassador from the African nation of Nigeria happened to step from the state banquet hall into the men's room at the same time. Standing at the urinals, the president glanced at the ambassador's member and couldn't help commenting: "I hope you don't think I'm rude, Mr. Ambassador, but I couldn't help noticing that what they say about black men having large penises is apparently true."

"Oh, no, Mr. President, that's just part of the mythos created between the races. If you want to have a penis as large as mine, all you have to do is before retiring each evening just give your penis a few whacks against the bedpost. This will increase its size."

"I'll certainly remember your advice, Mr. Ambassador."

Late that night when the official state banquet was finally over and the president was preparing to retire, he stopped at the foot of the bed in which the first lady was already asleep. Remembering what the ambassador from Nigeria had said, the president, feeling somewhat foolish, took his member in his hand and gave it a few tentative whacks on the bedpost. He experienced a quite pleasant tingling, somewhat smarting sensation in his member, so he gave it a few vigorous whacks against the bedpost.

From the depths of the bedcovers a sleepy first lady said, "Is that you, Mr. Ambassador?"

And God Created Woman

And God descended to the Garden of Eden to experience the wonders of his creation. He appeared unto Adam and asked, "Adam, I have given you the naming of the creatures of the land and waters and air."

"Yes, O Lord," replied Adam a little crankily, "and a wondrous lot of them there are, too. I'm naming them as fast as I can."

"This is good," said God unto Adam, "but I don't see the creature I created to be your soul mate, your partner in this beautiful garden."

"Oh, You mean Eve," said Adam.

"Eve," responded God, "what a lovely name you've chosen. Where is Eve?"

"I don't know," answered Adam, "this time of the month she's probably down at the river washing herself. She does that a lot."

"Oh, no," deplored God, "now I suppose all the fish are going to smell that way, too!"

College Boy

Ralphie received a long-distance phone call from his enraged father:

"How dare you write a check for fifty dollars to Pamela Sue Feelie and write 'Pussy' on it?! Are you nuts? What if your mother opened the bank statement instead of me? Do you want her to have a stroke?"

"Oh, Dad, come on, you know I like to have a good time, and you always said, 'You get what you pay for,' " replied Ralphie.

"Never goddamned mind what I always said. If you want to pay some cheap whore for a piece of ass, at least have the good sense to write something innocuous on the check like 'Nails.' "

"All right, all right, calm down, Dad. From now on I'll use 'Nails.' "

And the system worked. Ralphie didn't abuse his father's generosity, and every month there were several checks in varying amounts for nails.

And then one month there was a check in the amount of one hundred eighty dollars made out to Dr. V. Dee for "Repairs on the Hammer."

Back Street

On their wedding night Oscar asked his tender bride, "Darling, let's do it doggy-fashion first."

"Doggy-fashion? What do you think I am? A bitch?"

"No, no, no, my darling, my little kumquat pâté. It's just you know how much I adore your plump little derrière. I promise not to jump the channel and enter the wrong port."

"That does it, I'm leaving!"

"Precious, darling, sweetbreads, no, no, no, don't leave me in this state of erect acquiescence. I'll do it any way you say, but, my heart of hearts, if you want me to remember this moment the rest of my life, you'll let me do it to you doggy-fashion first."

"I don't have to whine and bark, do I?"

"No, no, no, my instant ecstasy, just moan and say, 'I love you.' "

"Well, all right."

"Ah, heaven-sent angel!"

"But we'll have to go to a street where nobody knows us!"

The Shot Heard Round the Bronx

Pauline was having a dinner for twelve and prided herself on doing all of the cooking. She worked very hard to get the dishes prepared just the way she liked them. A few minutes before the guests were to arrive, and with curlers still in her hair, she remembered the salad. "Oh, my God," she said, hurrying off to the kitchen. She diced, chopped, and shredded into a large salad bowl, then reached up into the cupboard for some of her special spices, but accidentally got hold of a box of BBs. "Oh, shit!" she said as she began to pick them out as fast as she could. The doorbell announced her first guest's arrival; she tossed the salad and raced to the door, stuffing her curlers into the umbrella stand in the foyer.

The dinner party was a great success and her cooking the hit of the evening.

The next morning her friend Sally called: "Pauline, again I must tell you what an excellently fabulous dinner you served last night. And to think it wasn't even catered, you did it all with your own two little hands. Nothing funny happened, did it?"

"Huh?" Pauline's smile of delight paling with apprehension.

"Nothing happened, did it? When you were fixing that delicious dinner, nothing unusual happened, did it?"

"What do you mean, 'unusual'? No, nothing unusual happened. Oh! The salad! I did forget about the salad and at the last minute was throwing a few things into the bowl and accidentally spilled some BBs. But I picked them all out."

"Like hell you did!" shouted Sally. "This morning I bent over, let a fart, and shot the canary!"

The James Boys

Old Jesse, Frank, and Henry were one fine train-robbing team. One crisp fall afternoon they boarded the woodburning *El Capitan* when it stopped for fuel. After the train was under way again, they systematically began going through the passenger cars. When they entered a car with pistols drawn, old Jesse would yell, "We're the James Boys. Stay in your seats and don't reach for your guns. We're going to rape all the women and rob all the men!"

"Just the cute ones, Jesse," Frank would giggle.

They were making a very nice living that fall afternoon, but by about the fourth car, Jesse was getting a little tired and yelled out, "We're the James Boys. Stay in your seats and don't reach for your guns. We're going to rob all the women and rape all the men!"

"Ah, Jesse," interrupted Frank. "Didn't you get that backward?"

A young man at the other end of the car shouted, "You shut up, Frank James, and let Mr. Jesse do just whatever he wants!"

Yankee Doodle

After finishing the fifth champagne cocktail Jerome had sent her, the well-stacked blonde perched at the end of the bar looked like she would take a tumble, so Jerome sidled over to her and asked, "My place or yours?"

"In a pig's ass," she slurred and passed out against his shoulder.

Jerome managed to get her out of the bar, into a taxi, up to his apartment, stripped and spread-eagled on his king-size bed. He quickly undressed, knelt between her legs, and slowly moved his hands up her creamy white thighs. His hands fairly tingled with excitement as they reached their destination, and his tongue involuntarily darted out, moistening his lips, as his thumbs slowly entered that delicious cavern he so yearned to explore. As he lowered his face to her and his thumbs parted those delicate pink inner lips, a little voice began to sing:

"Yankee Doodle went to town, riding on a pony . . ."

He leaped back as if slapped and stood mouth hanging open in shock and amazement. The singing had stopped. Shaking with disbelief, he again knelt between her legs and carefully opened her vagina.

"Stuck a feather in his hat, and called it macaroni . . ."

He removed his thumbs and the singing immediately stopped. Again he tried. Again the singing. Again it stopped when he removed his thumbs.

"I can't believe it. I can't fucking believe it!" he cried out loud. "It's incredible, what am I going to do?" He raced to the phone and dialed his friend Bernie. After too many rings, Bernie's sleepy voice finally answered. "Bernie, you're not going to believe this, Bernie, you've got to hear this," raved Jerome. "Hold on a minute." He placed the phone receiver on the blonde's stomach and slowly opened her vagina.

"Yankee Doodle went to town, riding on a pony. Stuck a feather in his hat, and called it macaroni," sang the little voice from within.

"Did you hear that, Bernie, did you hear it?" cried Jerome.

"Yeah, I heard it, you crazy son-of-a-bitch! What do you mean waking me up at three o'clock in the morning just to hear some silly cunt sing 'Yankee Doodle'!"

Fly the Friendly Skies

Two old friends were reunited coincidentally in the first-class cabin flying to the West Coast.

"My God, Cecily, where have you been?" asked Linda. "I haven't seen you in ages!"

"Oh, around, Linda dear," replied Cecily. "You know how it is, a week in Martinique, skiing at St. Moritz, London for the theater, Rome for the opera, just the ordinary. And you?"

"Oh, you know, about the same, minus the Martinique, St. Moritz, London, and Rome."

"Roger's business not doing well?"

"As well as usual. Rodney's hit the jackpot?"

"Well, not exactly, my dear, but I've taken this absolutely wonderful lover who gives me over a thousand a week just for mad money. You should take a lover, Linda dear. It'll open up new horizons for you."

"Yes, I suppose I should. Roger is practically married to his business anyway. But I probably wouldn't find one quite so generous as you have."

"Take two if they're small, I always say. Find two who'll each give you five hundred a week."

"And if I can't find two for five hundred?"

"Why then take four for one hundred twenty-five apiece."

"And if . . ."

A gentleman sitting across the aisle leaned over to them and said, "Pardon me, ladies, but I couldn't help overhearing your conversation. I'm going to sleep now, but wake me up when you get down to twenty bucks a throw!"

The Milkman Cometh

He's so gorgeous, thought Robin as she watched the brawny hunk swaying up the back walk. I've got a movie star for a milkman. At least a *Cosmo* centerfold. And why doesn't he wear any underwear? He must know I can see everything he's got. Careful, Robin, you're going to do something you'll never regret.

She opened the kitchen door and said, "Hi!"

"Wish I were," he answered, flashing her a smile that could have melted the polar ice cap.

"What's the matter," asked Robin, "your mom forget to wash your underwear?"

He involuntarily glanced down at his crotch, chuckled, and said, "Nah, I don't have any."

My God, she thought, look at it grow! And pulling up her dress, she said, "That's funny, neither do I."

She backed into the kitchen. He followed. In a tangle of lowered jeans, bared breasts, and passionate kisses, he elbowed the kitchen door closed and backed her against it, forcing his throbbing tool deep within her. Their spontaneous, avaricious lovemaking was thorough, grinding, and brief. He pulled out and pulled up his pants.

"Sorry, I've got to go. I've got more cream to deliver."

"Yeah, I'll bet you do," said Robin, still writhing and bucking against the door.

"What's the matter, didn't I give you enough?"

"Oh, sure, plenty," she replied. "It's just this goddamned doorknob's stuck up my ass!"

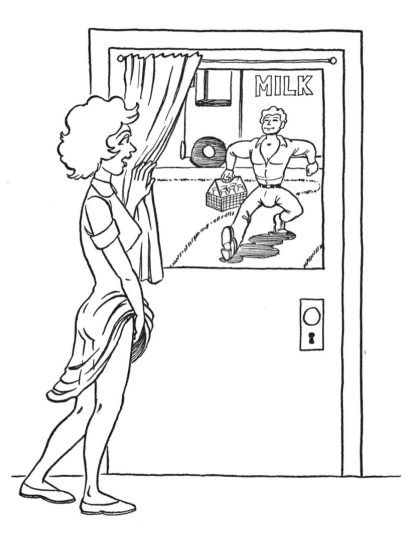

Breakfast with Molly T.

Molly T. went into the diner and ordered a bowl of oatmeal and a cup of plain tea. The waitress brought the oatmeal and tea. After a few mouthfuls of the oatmeal, Molly T. began rhapsodizing on how wonderful it was: "Oh, my goodness, this is the most wonderful oatmeal I've ever tasted in my life. Oh, waitress, I want to compliment you on your fantastic oatmeal. What is your secret?"

"Are you from the board of health?" asked the waitress.

"Good heavens, no! It's just your oatmeal is so special, you must have some secret ingredient. In fact, I think I've had it before, but I can't quite put my finger on that delicately tangy flavor."

"Well, if you do, let me know and I'll patent it," said the waitress.

After she finished her oatmeal, Molly T. called the waitress over and said, "Listen, I've just got to have another bowl of this superb oatmeal, so I can pin down that exquisite taste. I'm sure I've had it before. Sly puss, you could just tell me what it is, but, no, I would rather discover that feisty little flavor bud for myself. Please, another bowl of oatmeal."

"Hey, Ralphie, we've got a hot one here," called the waitress into the kitchen. "Come again on the oatmeal!"

"I knew it, I knew it!" cried Molly T. with instant recognition.

The Theater

Attending the British theater for the first time can be a bit perplexing for an American tourist, particularly when he's told there's no men's room, and he simply should go up to the balcony and do his business over the rail. Poor Mr. Randolph held his water as long as he could, then doubtfully made his way to the balcony, down the stairs through the crowded rows of theatergoers to the rail. No one paid any attention when he unzipped his fly, hung his member over the rail, and let go.

He flushed with the pleasure of relieving his bladder and thought with an amused grin that this was probably the most bizarre experience he would ever have. A stoic British voice from below in the orchestra called up.

"I say, old chap, would you mind bobbing it about a bit? I seem to be bearing the brunt of it!"

Piecemeal

Ah, the witching hour and Ben had an itch to get a little comfort and pleasure from one of the fair sex. He was desperate to get laid. She looked soft and lovely standing under the streetlamp. At least she didn't look diseased, and Ben was cheap and she was cheap, so off they went to the dingy hotel room where she worked.

She left the lights turned low and quickly slipped out of her dress, knocking off her wig and exposing a sparsely covered pate. She slipped off her bra, and her enormous bazooms came away with it. She removed her hip-length boots. Her left leg went with the boot. She popped her false teeth into a glass of water, stretched back over the bed in her most alluring pose, and said, "Come and get it, big boy."

All Ben could think of was dog food as he turned and fled toward the door.

"What's the matter, big boy?" she called out after him. "Can't you get it up?"

"Sorry," answered Ben. "I must have left my prick in my other pair of pants!"

Hangman, Spare That Tree

A very beautiful but severely crippled young girl met a man one day who drove her out to a lovers' lane in the woods. When their amiable chatter soon turned to heavy kissing and petting, she told him, "If you want to make love to me, I have a hook in the back of my dress. All you have to do is hang me on a low tree branch."

A bit taken aback but not wishing to displease her, he did as requested and hung her on a tree branch she selected for its bounce and sway. Then he proceeded to ravish her to their hearts' content.

After they were both exhausted from their sexual play, he unhooked her from the tree branch, carried her back to the car, and began the drive back to town.

She placed her hand on his leg as he drove and said, "I'm very proud that you've chosen me to spend the rest of your life with."

"What?" he said, aghast at the thought.

"It must have been a heavy decision for you to make, but believe me, it's the right one."

"What are you talking about?"

"Oh, aren't you sweet? Love, my darling, love!"

"Love?"

"And I love you, too."

"I never said I loved you!"

"But you do, I just know you do."

"But I don't!"

"Yes, you do."

"Oh no, I don't!"

"But you have to. You must."

"Why? Why must I?"

"Because you're the only one who ever unhooked me from the tree branch afterward!"

Hillbilly Boy

Young Hillbilly Boy came down out of the Ozark Mountains to find himself a job and landed in this small town where a circus was playing. He'd always heard of the glitter of circus life and thought it would be a real fine idea to get a job with the circus, so he went to the circus manager.

"Well, Boy, you look a little green to me," said the circus manager. "Ever work in a circus before?"

"No, sir."

"Don't think I've got much of a job for you then, except maybe tending and feeding the lions."

"Lions?" gulped Hillbilly Boy. "I don't think I could get near a lion. I'd be too skeered."

"Sure, you could. Come on, I'll show you how it's done."

The circus manager took Hillbilly Boy to the lion's cage and picked up a bucket of meat on the way.

"You see, first you open the door to the cage like this. And then you just throw in the meat, close the cage, and that's it."

"Well, what if the lion comes at me when I open the door?"

"Just stare him in the eye. He'll back down."

"And what if he don't?"

"Then throw some shit in his face."

"Shit? Where am I gonna get some shit?"

"Reach around in the back of your pants. You'll find plenty!"

Cock of the Walk

Farmer Prufrock's old rooster, Chanticleer, had been ruling the roost for a mighty long time, so the good farmer bought a second cock, a big, sassy, young fellow he named Rocky and set loose in the barnyard with the encouragement, "Go for it!"

Old Chanticleer stalked up to Rocky and said in a conciliatory way, "I'm a little worn out, you know, past my prime, and I don't want a fight. There are over two hundred chicks here. Listen, what do you say, just leave me a dozen or so, huh, buddy?"

"No way, chicken shit," replied Rocky. "It's Colonel Sanders time for you."

"Hold up a minute there, young fellow," begged Chanticleer. "Give me a chance to go the distance. Race me as far as the barn, give me a yard start, and if you win, I'll deep-fat myself. Only a yard start, come on, what do you say, how 'bout it?"

"Stop, stop, you're breakin' my heart. All right, a yard and I'll spot you two more. Start running, extra crispy!"

Old Chanticleer took off for the barn. Rocky puffed up a bit for the biddies, then took off like a shot after the old rooster. But suddenly there's another shot, and Rocky dropped in his tracks, dead as last year's contender.

"I'll be ding-donged," said Farmer Prufrock breaking open his shotgun. "That's the third cock I've bought in two weeks, and every dang one of them turned out to be queer!"

Assume the Position

"I don't want to have a baby!"

"Now, Mrs. Wade, it's too late for that kind of talk. You're in your sixth month and having a fine pregnancy."

"That's easy for you to say! I'm the one who looks like a toad!"

"Now, dear, you've only put on the weight an expectant mother should, not a pound more."

"But I'm sick every morning. I hate it!"

"Mrs. Wade, I told you about morning sickness. It's just one of the little crosses an expectant mother must bear."

"I'll never get my figure back!"

"With the right diet and exercise, of course you will."

"My husband doesn't love me anymore!"

"Did he say that?"

"Of course the idiot didn't say it! But he treats me like I'm going to break or something. I know he can't stand to touch me."

"He's just concerned for you. Many husbands over-react to the delicacy of their wife's condition."

"Humpf! A fat lot you care!"

"Mrs. Wade, I've tried to help you in every way I can. You're going to have a fine baby. In three months this will all be over, and you'll be a very proud mother. Now, do you have any questions?"

"Yes, what position will I have to be in when the baby comes?"

"In approximately the same position as when you conceived it."

"Oh, my God! You mean I have to ride around in a rowboat for two hours with my legs dangling over the side, too?!"

Fly Away

Sister Mary Michael was at it again. This time she was chasing the birds out of the convent vegetable garden by running up and down the neatly tended rows, flailing her arms about, and crying, "Fuck off! Fuck off!"

Her cries even reached Mother Superior's office. Mother Superior was a patient woman, but this was too much even for her. She dashed out to the garden and said, "Sister Mary Michael! Stop shouting that obscenity this instant! Get over here. Now!"

Sister Mary Michael, totally abashed by the tone of Mother Superior's voice, hung her head and did as she was told.

"Sister Mary Michael, what am I to do with you? We simply cannot have that kind of language in our convent. Now can we?"

"No, Mother Superior."

"If you want the little birdies to fly away, just say, 'Shoo! Shoo!' They'll fuck off!"

The Fireman's Ball

The five-alarmer had been raging out of control for hours, pouring thick smoke over the street and making reconnaisance and keeping track of the firefighting forces difficult. At last the blaze seemed to be beaten into submission and the mopping-up operations were under way. The fire captains were reporting to the chief of operations the condition of their men and equipment. Captain Clancey had accounted for all of his men but two, Firemen Jones and Kelly.

Captain Clancey rounded the fire truck blocking the entrance to the alley, and there was young Fireman Jones, with his pants down around his ankles, leaning over a trash can being buggered roundly by Fireman Kelly.

"My God!" exhorted Captain Clancey. "What the

devil do you think you're doing here?"

"He passed out, smoke inhalation, sir," gasped Fireman Kelly plunging in and out of Fireman Jones. "I'm giving him treatment."

"Smoke inhalation? Good God, man, you're supposed to be giving him mouth-to-mouth resuscitation!"

"Yeah, I know, Captain. That's what led us to this!"

Hopscotch Crotch

"Honey, what's this underwear doing on the floor of my closet?"

"I don't know, sweetheart, you probably threw it there."

"But I don't wear this kind, I wear—"

"Boxers. Well, you've got me, love, maybe you picked them up on a business trip?"

"Honey, what's this lipstick doing all over the crotch of these shorts?"

"Oops."

"Oops?"

"Well . . ."

"Oops? Well? I find another man's underwear in the bottom of my closet with lipstick all over the crotch, and all you can say is 'Oops? Well?' "

"*Merde.*"

"*Merde?!* All right, who was it?!"

"Who was what, dear?"

"Don't give me that crap! Who was it? Was it Gibson?!"

"No."

"Who, then? Davis?!"

"No."

"Wolfe?"

"No, no, no!"

"What's the matter, deep throat—none of my friends good enough for you?!"

Cockney Lass

A cockney girl from London visiting America for the first time was being driven absolutely crazy by her American relatives, who constantly harassed her about pronouncing her *H*s. Finally she became so fed up with their relentless nagging, she told them, "Aw, to 'ell with the lot of you. I'm going for a walk."

Being a lass who enjoyed long walks and since the day was so bright, breezy, and pleasant, her mood soon became happy again, and she walked all the way to the Brooklyn Bridge. As she strolled across the bridge, her aversion to wearing panties allowed her to enjoy the delightful sensation of the playful breezes on her bare and tender span. She soon came abreast of a young patrolman, whose eyes almost popped out of his head when her dress billowed up and around her.

Liking what he saw and being a brash young American patrolman to boot, he ventured to strike up a conversation with her.

"A bit airy down there, isn't it?"

"What'd you expect?" she snapped back. "Ostrich feathers?!"

The Homecoming

Hunnicunt pulled into his driveway returning home from a selling trip and gave the customary two beeps on the car horn to announce his arrival. He parked the car in the garage, hopped out, and headed for the house. But no adorable wifey came tripping lightly out to meet him with open arms and the laughter of reunion. His mood changed as he heard the loud music coming from within. This was certainly unlike his wife. He let himself in the back door.

"Honey, I'm home!" he called, but no responding

joyful greeting came from his loving spouse. He headed toward the upstairs and the loud music, which he followed to his own bedroom. He paused a moment at the door, that moment when any husband might have the unwanted flash of doubt, opened the door, and walked in. There was the light of his life in bed with the handsome young doctor who had just moved into the neighborhood.

"What's going on here?!" he exploded.

"Mr. Hunnicunt! Well, you see . . ."

"Harry!"

"Well, you see, your wife had a slight fever, and I'm taking her temperature," caged the young doctor.

Seeing the lie, but wanting to believe it, Hunnicunt paused a moment, then said, "Doctor, I don't want to call you a liar, but when you pull that thing out of her, it sure as hell better have numbers on it!"

Chlorophyll

"Good afternoon, Mr. Little. Did my chlorophyll soap come in? You asked me to check back this morning."

"Just let me see. We got part of our order yesterday, and the balance is due this afternoon. Hmmm, no, Tim didn't check it off. It must be coming in this afternoon's shipment."

"Oh, drat."

"Could I interest you in another brand?"

"No, I'm sorry, I've tried them all, and this one's the only one I'm not allergic to. I use it for my personal hygiene. Do you understand? My very personal, feminine hygiene."

"Ah, I see. Could you drop by this afternoon?"

"No, that won't be possible. I'll ask my husband to stop in after work. You can't miss him. He's the tall man with the brown hair and the green mustache."

The Midas Touch

"You have a beautiful baby boy," said the nurse as she placed the tiny bundle in the mother's arms.

It wasn't until later at home when the new mother was changing her baby boy's diaper for the first time that she noticed the gold screw in his navel. She started, then took a second look, a second, long, long look. There it was in his tiny innie navel, a gold screw.

"Now, there's nothing to worry about," said her doctor when she called him. "Yes, we noticed it, but didn't want to upset you at the time. Well, not exactly ... well, actually, no. I've never seen anything like it before. No, there are no records of any baby ever having been born before with a gold screw in its navel. We decided to leave well enough alone and not to mention it to anyone. You know how the press might take off. No, don't try to take it out. Somehow it seems so natural to him, don't you think?"

The baby boy was raised to think nothing either way about the gold screw. He didn't even notice it much. After all, he did have an innie navel. Once when he did examine it and became curious, his mother told him never, never ever take it out, and that was that.

On the night of his eighteenth birthday, after a wonderful party and a great evening, he lay in his bed picking at the gold screw and decided to remove it. With his little-fingernail he began turning it bit by bit until it came away in his hand. Nothing happened. He sighed with relief and fell asleep.

But the next morning when he hopped out of bed, his ass fell off!

Their First Ballet

"Ooo-eeee!" said Tyrone after the ballet was over. "Did you see how that ballerina could dance, the way she leaped and twirled? Did you see how she got up on her toes and took those itty-bitty steps back and forth, and the way she stood up on one toe and pointed the other one up in the air?"

"Shut your mouth, Tyrone," replied Jasmine, "or I'll point your chin up in the air with my fist!"

"What's the matter with you?"

"I saw the way your eyeballs crawled all over that poor skinny little child, tryin' to pry their way under that tutu she was wearing."

"Don't jump on me, Jasmine. You told me to develop an appreciation for the fine arts."

"Fine arts, my eye. I didn't notice you payin' no mind to those sissy boys up there with their behinds crackin' open like an old whore's smile every step they took."

"The ballerina's the main thing. They're just there to make her look good."

"Look good? That flat-chested, bony little mess? You want someone to look good, I'll show you lookin' good."

So Jasmine made Tyrone hang behind all the others, and when the auditorium was cleared, she said, "Now boost me up on this stage and I'll show you lookin' good."

He boosted her up on the stage, and she kicked off her shoes, hoisted up her skirt, and danced. She leaped, twirled, spun, bounded, and, for a grand finale, she landed in a set of splits that made poor Tyrone's groin ache.

"All right, all right, Jasmine, you were lookin' fine, finer than that ballerina ever could look."

"Humph! I thought so," snorted Jasmine in triumph. "Now slide me over to the side of the stage so I can break the suction and we can get out of here."

The Latest Thing

"I'm sorry, Frances, but the rabbit died," reported the doctor.

"What?"

"The rabbit died, the frog croaked, it's rubber-baby-buggy-bumper time for you. You're preggers, deary."

"What?! I don't believe it. No! No! No! Why you old son-of-a-bitch! What do you mean I'm pregnant?!"

"You know, big stomach, throwing up in the morning, nine months of ugly fat, pregnant!"

"I'll kill you, you cocky bastard! You know, guts strewn all over the street, feet in concrete in the East River, six feet under, kill you!"

"Now, now, Frances, I warned you. You want to play, you got to pay," stammered the doctor.

"I've got to pay? You're the one who's going to pay! I asked you for some protection, and all you gave me were those damn little pills!"

"I don't understand it. They're the latest thing!"

"Latest thing, my rosy-red keester," screamed Frances. "Every time I stood up, the damn thing fell out on the floor!"

Really, Rodney

Cecily's husband arrived home unexpectedly one afternoon and caught Cecily playing horsy-horsy on a business acquaintance's sanguine steed.

"Bitch!" he roared. "Slut! Daughter of a slut! Granddaughter of a slut! Great-granddaughter of a—"

"Can it, Rodney!" snapped Cecily. "You've got a lot

of nerve slamming in here like Attila the Hun. Let's get a few things straight, Rodney darling. Just who do you think floated that stock merger when your firm was about to go down the toilet? Who do you think paid the bill for my tummy tuck you admired so much, and who do you think paid your sanitarium bills this spring when you had the DT's and had to dry out? You wouldn't have a pot to piss in or a window to throw it out of if it weren't for Mr. McGee here. So just watch your mouth! And where do you think you're sneaking off to?!"

"Nowhere, sweetums, I was just going to close the window. We wouldn't want Mr. McGee to catch a draft, would we?"

Hickory, Dickory, Dock

Little Tommy burst into his parents' bedroom without knocking late one night after being awakened by a nightmare. His mother and father moved quickly, but not before Tommy's bright little eyes saw his mother's open nakedness as she snatched at the covers, and not before Tommy's bright little eyes saw his father's erect penis in one hand and the open jar of petroleum jelly in the other. Tommy's father dropped to his knees on the floor and he busily pretended to search around under the bed.

Any recollection of the nightmare vanished quickly from Tommy's mind, and he asked, "What ya doing?"

"Ah, Tommy," said his father, "I'm glad you came in just when you did. Your mommy saw a mouse run under the bed, and I'm trying to find it."

"What ya going to do when you find it?" asked Tommy innocently. "Fuck it?"

Taxi!

A respectable family man was cabbing up Eighth Avenue in New York City with his little daughter when she noticed all the ladies on the street.

"Daddy, who are all those ladies in the short skirts swinging their handbags and waving at the cars?"

"Well, princess, those ladies are just waiting for their husbands to get off work and come out of their offices."

"Don't you believe it, little girl," said the cab driver. "Those ladies are all two-bit whores lookin' to French some asshole for a fin. And if your daddy were an honest man, he'd tell you the truth."

"Daddy," asked the little girl, "what are two-bit whores looking to French some asshole for a fin?"

"Well, princess . . . those are ladies who have more than one husband. Sometimes they have many husbands."

"Gee, Daddy, with all those husbands, they must have an awful lot of children. What do they do with all of them?"

"Well, princess, I expect they raise them to be New York City cab drivers," he answered sweetly.

Chicken Little

Chicken Little was pecking away at something really nasty in the barnyard when a great big chicken hawk swooped down, gobbled him up, and swallowed him down in one big gulp without even missing a wing beat, and soared away into the bright blue sky. That's the last thing Chicken Little remembered until he squeezed his head out the chicken hawk's rear end and cried, "The sky is falling! The sky is falling!"

"No, it's not, dummy!" said the chicken hawk. "You've just been eaten by a chicken hawk, that's all." And he gave Chicken Little a little squeeze around the neck with his sphincter just to convince him of the truth of it.

Chicken Little looked down from the dizzying height and said, "My goodness, we sure are high up. How high up are we?"

"Oh, about fifteen thousand feet, I reckon."

"Fifteen thousand feet? Fifteen thousand feet?! You wouldn't be shittin' me now, would you?!"

A Nun's Story

Caring for the poor and sick often took Sister Mary Michael into some of the seedier sections of town. One night, returning to the convent, she was snatched off a dimly lit derelict street into a dismally dark alley and raped. After the rape her assailant rolled off her and lay panting in the darkness. Just then a car turned the corner and for a moment the automobile headlights reflected off the alley wall, and the rapist realized he had just brutalized a nun.

"Oh, my God, Sister," said the rapist, "what have I done? Why didn't you tell me you're a nun? Oh, no, I'm so sorry."

Poor little Sister Mary Michael just lay there, her habit all askew, sniffling quietly.

"Oh, Sister, please, don't cry. I'm sorry, I would never have. . . . What are you going to do? What are you going to say to the Father Confessor? You'll have to tell him about this at confession."

"I'll just tell him I was raped . . . twice," sniffled Sister Mary Michael.

"Twice?"

"Well, if you're not too tired," she answered.

106

Miss Pimm's Revenge

"It's my microwave," said Miss Pimm. "I need a screw for the door of my microwave. It's just hanging there by one screw. The other one popped out and bounced across my kitchen counter into the sink and down the drain."

"You ought to keep your drain stopper in. This kind of thing wouldn't happen," said the hardware-store owner. "It's not my fault you lost your screw."

"I didn't say it was your fault, Mr. Anderson. All I said was—"

"I heard what you said. What size screw you need?"

"Not a very big one."

"Oh, fine, just fine," said Mr. Anderson. "Smaller than a breadbox, I suppose? What kind of microwave do you have?"

Just then, Mr. Anderson's son, Harry, poked his head through the door to the little office at the back of the store.

"Pop, Mom's on the phone, wants to talk to you about some weed killer," he said, then disappeared back into the office.

"Weed killer, weed killer, that's all I hear. I'm surprised there's anything left alive in that damn yard with all her sprays and pellets," said Mr. Anderson as he headed for the office.

"What about my screw?" called Miss Pimm after him.

"I'll give you a screw!" Mr. Anderson muttered under his breath. Harry came to help Miss Pimm.

"My, my, my, little Harry? Is that you? All grown up and home from college for the summer?"

"Yes, ma'am, Miss Pimm, it's me. Pop says you want a screw for a microwave."

Miss Pimm looked her former nemesis straight in the eye and said, "No, but I'll blow you for that toaster over there!"

C'est la Guerre

During World War II when the Nazis were stamping their loathsome swastikas across Europe and Africa, the Führer issued the edict that all enlisted men were to rape as many women as possible in all captured villages, towns, and cities. After the rape, the enlisted man was to stand, give the Nazi salute, and announce: "In nine months you will have a baby. Name it Adolf. Heil Hitler!"

One particularly puny German soldier hadn't raped a single woman. His commanding officer and fellow enlisted men were giving him such a hard time, sniping at his German manhood, his duty to Führer and Fatherland, and his natural Aryan superiority, that one night he determinedly set out to rape the first woman he met who was not too large or too robust. In the occupied French village he came across such a frail girl with such a plaintive and forlorn look about her that he couldn't resist raping her on the spot for Führer and Fatherland. After the rape he stood, clicked his heels, shot his right arm up stiff in the Nazi salute, and said: "In nine months you will have a baby. Name it Adolf. Heil Hitler!"

To which she replied: "In three days, you will have a disease. Name it syphilis. *Vive la France!*"

Sex Convention

"And now, ladies and gentlemen, that we've heard our esteemed guest speakers' opening remarks, and before we break up into our discussion groups, I'd like to try a little experiment. As an indication of the wide range of sexual experience represented at this convention, please stand up for a moment when I name the category you think you best fit. Those of you who have sex at least once a night, please stand."

A goodly number of the assembly stood, and an appreciative murmur was heard.

"Those of you who have sex at least once a week, please stand." A larger portion stood.

"Those who have sex at least once a month?" A smaller portion rose from their seats.

"At least once every three months?" Fewer stood.

"At least once every six months?" Very few stood.

"At least once a year?" Only one fellow toward the back jumped from his seat, joyously waving his hand at the speaker and dancing up and down. A nervous titter ran through the crowd, and many had to cover their mouths to suppress their laughter.

"Excuse me, sir," said the speaker. "I don't mean to be rude, but I can't help noticing how overjoyed you are to have sex only once a year. Might I ask why?"

"Because tonight's the night!" shouted the fellow ecstatically.

A Chip Off the Old Block

"Cherie!" called Mrs. Lipshitz from her boudoir. "Come in here a moment, please."

"Yes, Mrs. Lipshitz?"

"Cherie, how long have you been with us now?"

"Three and a half months, ma'am."

"Three and a half months. Certainly long enough to work into a new situation, wouldn't you say?"

"Yes, ma'am."

"Well, you haven't."

"What?"

"I'm sorry, but I don't believe in giving warnings. It just makes the help sneakier."

"Sneakier?!"

"I'm going to have to fire you, Cherie. You're a lousy housekeeper and cook."

"But Mrs. Lipshitz, I'm a better cook than you are!"

"Who told you that?"

"Your husband did."

"Oh, did he. I'm afraid I won't be able to give you a letter of reference either."

"And I'm far better in bed than you are!"

"I suppose my husband told you that, too, did he?"

"No, Mrs. Lipshitz, he didn't. Your son did!"

Three Little Pigs

"Hey, bartender, set us up another round here! I want to tell old Charlie about the time I diddled those three girlies down by Bull Crick. And I know old Charlie's gonna need somethin' cool and refreshin' to keep him from overheatin' his self and stickyin' up his britches."

"Aw, shut up, Jim, I ain't done that since I was in high school."

"When was you ever in high school, you lyin' jack-ass!"

"Sheeet."

"Well, like I was sayin', I was down to Bull Crick fishin' when these pretty little darlin's came splashin' around bare-assed like three shiny little minnows. Then I started fishin' for real, only I switched poles and let 'em get a good look when I took a leak on the crick bank. Honest to God, one of them girls came splashin' right up the bank and grabbed ahold of my pole and pulled me into the bushes."

"Sheeet."

"I gave her such a screwin' I thought my heart would break. And then you know what? She jumped up and turned a somersault in the air. Claimed it guaranteed she wouldn't catch the seed and get pregnant."

"Sheeet."

"You know, Jim, old buddy, for the rest of that afternoon I had one on the ground and two in the air every damn minute!"

"Awwwwwwww."

When Knights Were Bold

King Arthur had to make a long journey but loathed to leave his lovely Queen Guinevere in Camelot. His experience told him not to trust any of his Knights of the Round Table with his lovely, lonely wife, so he had Merlin, his magician, devise a cunning chastity belt, to which only Arthur had the key. This clever device would allow a trespassing penis to enter, but would chop it off with a tiny guillotine concealed within.

Girding Guinevere with the chastity belt and swearing his knights to an oath of loyalty, Arthur bid them a fond farewell and set out on his journey. It was several months later before he again saw the walls of Camelot.

"Now that my journey has been a success, and before we begin the celebration feast, I have one more thing to ask of you. Would you all please lower your pants, so I may inspect each in turn to ascertain if any of you have been unloyal to me and have tried to dally with my Guinevere."

This created quite a stir, but since Arthur had unsheathed Excalibur as he made his request, the knights meekly lowered their pants for inspection. Poor Arthur was distraught almost to desperation as he inspected the line of hacked and mutilated penises. At the end of the line stood Lancelot, the only knight with his penis intact.

"Ah, Lancelot, faithful Lancelot!" rejoiced Arthur. "One shining knight among this pack of scoundrels. Upon you I will heap bounty and lands equal to that which I scourge from these other scabby jackals. What do you have to say to that, loyal Lancelot?"

And Lancelot replied, "Mawawrgghh!"

The Cocktail Party

"Cecily, what a glittering array of personalities you've gathered in one room," chirruped her friend Linda. "There's Mailer and Cavett, Mischa and Natasha, Merv and Johnny, or is that Martini and Rossi? It's so thrilling, I'll be namedropping for absolutely weeks!"

"So charmed you could come, Linda dear."

"Oh my God, who is that?"

"Where, dear?"

"Over by the ice seal splashing around in caviar. Who's that hideously ugly man?"

"Tut, tut, Linda, dear, he's a very promising poet. Writes all about being victimized, very *au courant,* don't you think?"

"But his face!"

"Believe me, dear, under all that acne, the scars, the missing eye—isn't he just too-too, refusing to wear a patch?—beats the heart of a very sensitive human being."

Later in the evening our hostess, Cecily, disappeared, and strangely enough, so did the ugly but promising poet. Linda instigated a one-woman search. She searched the main floor, the upstairs, and finally on an ancient brass bed up in the attic found our hostess Cecily trying to swallow the eyeless poet's whang.

"Cecily! Ughh!" shrieked Linda in disgust. "How could you?!"

"Really, darling, anything to get away from that face!"

Randy Randy

"Hello, Doc Fields? This is Farmer Prufrock here. This morning I bought this pretty little filly over at the horse auction. She's as sleek as a whistle, and I plan to race her this comin' season. Well, my problem is that old stallion Randy's been brayin' his durn head off like a jackass ever since he smelled her on the place, and she's just gonna have to be in the corral with him tonight 'til I can fence off a space for her in the mornin'. I don't want her gettin' knocked up or she won't be able to race. Do what? Tie a bedsheet around her rump? You're sure? You're sure you're sure? You are. I am. Sorry to have troubled you."

Bright and early the next morning Farmer Prufrock was up and out to the corral to see if the bedsheet chastity belt had stayed in place, but his new filly was nowhere in sight. He trailed her over to a neighboring farm and asked a fieldhand if he'd seen a filly run by with a bedsheet tied around her rump.

"No," answered the fieldhand. "But I saw one dash past 'bout twenty minutes ago with a hanky stickin' out of her ass!"

One-night Stand

"I know I should have told you before we left the bar, but I was afraid you wouldn't want me."

"Oh, baby, how could you say that? Of course I want you. What was your name again?"

"Darlene."

"Yeah, sure, Darlene, the prettiest name I can think of."

"But I don't have sex like other girls, I mean, well, I only like to get fucked by a guy's big toe."

"Luckily I had a pedicure the other day. We're going to have a swell time, Doreen."

"Darlene."

"Yeah, sure, Darlene."

Several days later: "Doctor, I just don't understand it. My big toe swelled up twice its normal size, and now it's split open and draining some yellow gunk all the time."

"Nothing to worry about. A couple million units of biocillin and it'll clear up. The blood tests show it's syphilis of the big toe. I've treated stranger."

"Stranger than syphilis of the big toe?"

"Sure, just this morning I treated a young woman for athlete's vagina."

Merry Christmas!

"Ho, ho, ho!" said Santa as he slid down the chimney with his bag of goodies. He stepped from the fireplace into the arms of a statuesque naked brunette.

"Merry Christmas, Santa. I'm your present, all unwrapped and ready for love. Won't you spend the night with me?"

"Ho, ho, ho, gotta go!" replied Santa. "It's Christmas Eve, you know!"

And strangely enough, the next chimney he slid down led him into the arms of a voluptuous blonde, also naked.

"Here comes Santa Claus, here comes Santa Claus," she sang. "And I hope you do, all night long with me."

"Ho, ho, ho, gotta go!" replied Santa. "It's Christmas Eve, you know!"

And when Santa slid down the next chimney, he peeped cautiously from the fireplace. And there, spread like a satyr's feast, was the most beautiful redhead with the biggest bazookas he'd ever seen. Always partial to redheads with big bazookas, he stopped short and caught his breath. In spite of the urgency of his mission that night, Santa felt that old swelling in his pants testing the seams.

"Hey, little old elf, so spritely and quick," said the redhead, "step over here, and I'll give it a lick!"

To which Santa replied, "Hey, hey, hey, better stay! Can't get up the chimney now anyway!"

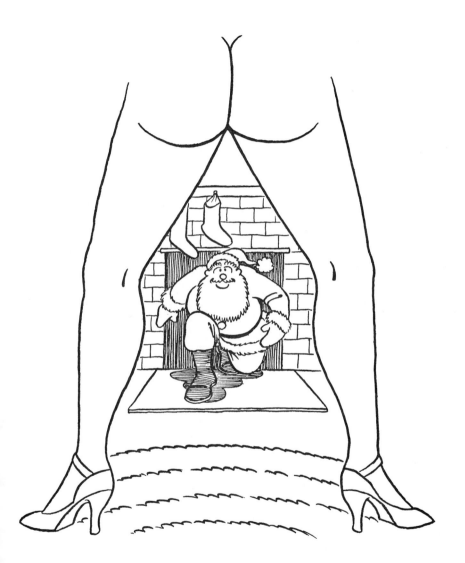

Dirty Dave and Baby Jesus

When old Dirty Dave was a little boy, he asked his mother for pencil and paper so he could write to Santa Claus for lots of wonderful Christmas presents.

"You've been so bad this year, Santa Claus isn't going to listen to you," said his mother. "You'd do better to write to the Baby Jesus."

"Dear Baby Jesus," wrote little Dave, "I want lots of wonderful Christmas presents, and I promise to be good for a whole year."

Realizing he could never be good for a whole year, little Dave tore up that letter and wrote:

"Dear Baby Jesus, I want lots of wonderful Christmas presents, and I promise to be good for a whole month."

Realizing he could never be good for a whole month, he tore up that letter and wrote:

"Dear Baby Jesus, I want lots of wonderful Christmas presents, and I promise to be good for a whole day."

Realizing he couldn't be good for even one whole day, little Dirty Dave tore up that letter, went into his mother's room, got the statue of the Madonna, wrapped it in brown paper, tied it up with string, and hid it in the desk drawer. Then he wrote:

"Dear Baby Jesus, if you ever want to see your mother alive again . . ."